"This invaluable new resource gave me a better understanding of the whole process. Anybody with an interest in this subject should read this – to learn how it is done."

> — Joel Simon, Producer, *The Marine*, *X-Men*,
> *The In-Laws*, *The Wild, Wild West*, *Hard To Kill*

"Michele Wallerstein offers up what so few writers have but genuinely need: business sense. You may not agree with everything in this book, and you may not like to hear it... but it'll definitely give you a sense of what goes through agents' heads as they read your work or evaluate your pitch."

> — Chad Gervich, Writer/Producer, *Wipeout*, *Speeders*,
> *Foody Call*; Author, *Small Screen, Big Picture: A Writer's
> Guide to the TV Business*

"In *Mind Your Business*, veteran lit agent Michele Wallerstein gives you a perspective another writer won't. Minding your busines – and agenting your agent – is almost as important as your screenwriting craft. When I was starting out, Ms. Wallerstein was one of the agents people recommended I contact. She really knows her stuff. Check it out."

> — Alex Epstein, Screenwriter, *Bon Cop/Bad Cop*, *Naked
> Josh*; Author, *Crafty Screenwriting*;
> Blogger, Complications Ensue

"One of the most insightful and helpful books I've ever read about writing for TV and film and the entertainment business in general. I only wish it had been published when I was starting out in the business."

> — Chuck Gordon, Producer, *Hitman*, *October Sky*,
> *Unlawful Entry*, *K-9*, *Waterworld*, *Die Hard*

"In *Mind Your Business*, former agent Michele Wallerstein gives screenwriters an inside look at navigating the rough waters of Tinseltown!"

> — Kathie Fong Yoneda, Author, *The Script-Selling Game*

"At last, a book that makes the business of Hollywood understandable and accessible (and less frightening). Spending time with Michele and this book can help any writer who wants a writing career – and wants to learn how to make it happen."

> — Dr. Linda Seger, Script Consultant; Author, *Making a
> Good Script Great, And the Best Screenplay Goes To...*

"Any screenwriter who thinks he or she knows what an agent 'should do' should read Michele Wallerstein's straightforward book – a veteran agent's glimpse into how the film world actually wheels and deals. Do yourself a favor, and learn what an agent can and can't do – and why."

> — Mary J. Schirmer, Screenwriter; Instructor;
> Co-President of *Screenplayers.net*

"A must-read for writers wanting to break into the business and a good reference for industry professionals. It's fun, honest and informative, with no frills, like Wallerstein herself."

— Madeline DiMaggio, Author, *How To Write for Television*;
Writer, Producer, and Consultant

"Loved this book! Michele Wallerstein's book delivers on its promise, offering expert advice and insightful anecdotes from a seasoned insider who truly knows the game and how to play it."

— Lisa Lieberman Doctor, former motion picture
Development Executive; Writers Guild Award
nominee; Writing Instructor

"*Mind Your Business* is a practical, no-nonsense guide for writers navigating the film industry. It covers a broad range of topics, from money to meetings to contracts – and contains a lot of helpful advice for writers just getting started. Get inside the mind of an agent!"

— Amanda Pendolino, *http://aspiringtvwriter.blogspot.com*

"If you're serious about your screenwriting career and looking for the real skinny on agents, then this book is the perfect addition to your library. As every professional knows, if the business side of your writing isn't working, the creative side will never flourish."

— Robert Grant, Sci-Fi-London, *www.sci-fi-london.com*

"*Mind Your Business* fills in the missing puzzle pieces for screenwriters. It not only offers great tips to absorb before writing a script, but also provides essential tools for thriving in Hollywood *after* you've gotten an agent. Finally there's a book that sheds light on the realities of the agent/writer relationship, the business of screenwriting, and the approach necessary to succeed in Hollywood."

— Trevor Mayes, Writer, Owner of *www.Scriptwrecked.com*

"*Mind Your Business* gives a look at a side of the screenwriting world that isn't often covered in straight 'art of screenwriting' books. As a Hollywood literary agent, Wallerstein can give tips that other authors can't – especially by covering those 'unwritten' business rules writers usually discover as they go along."

— Erin Corrado, *www.onemoviefiveviews.com*

A Hollywood Literary Agent's Guide
To Your Writing Career

MIND
YOUR
BUSINESS

- - - - - - - -

Michele Wallerstein

Published by Michael Wiese Productions
12400 Ventura Blvd. # 1111
Studio City, CA 91604
tel. 818.379.8799
fax 818.986.3408
mw@mwp.com
www.mwp.com

Cover Design: MWP
Interior Book Design: Gina Mansfield Design
Editor: Gary Sunshine

Printed by McNaughton & Gunn, Inc., Saline, Michigan
Manufactured in the United States of America

Library of Congress Cataloging-in-Publication Data

Wallerstein, Michele
 Mind your business : a Hollywood literary agent's guide to your writing
career / Michele Wallerstein.
    p. cm.
 Includes index.
 ISBN 978-1-932907-76-6
 1. Motion picture authorship. I. Title.
 PN1996.W235 2010
 808'.066791--dc22
                                        2010001873

Mixed Sources
Product group from well-managed
forests and other controlled sources
www.fsc.org Cert no. SW-COC-002283
FSC © 1996 Forest Stewardship Council

To my husband, Gregg Weiss

- - - - - - -

The idea guy, the love of my life,
and the smartest
and the funniest man I know

CONTENTS

ACKNOWLEDGMENTS

First and foremost I want thank Natalie Moses, who has been my friend, supporter, and secret-keeper, and who has given me unconditional love since we were in the Brownies. Without her I would never have made it through the trials and tribulations of my life.

A special appreciation is due to the people in the screenplay-consulting field who have welcomed me with open arms and shared their knowledge, insights, information, and friendship. To Donie Nelson, Rona Edwards, Maddie DiMaggio, Michael Hauge, Paul Chitlik, Monika Skerbelis, Linda Seger, and Kathie Fong-Yoneda, thank you all from the bottom of my heart.

To the great Mollie Gregory, a terrific writer and former president of Women in Film, who taught me how to lead, how to write, and how to be patient, and who has always been so generous and kind.

A special thank you to the Writers Guild of America and Chuck Slocum for their cooperation in helping with this book.

Thank you to Dr. David Clark, whose wisdom and support brought me back into the light.

And, lastly, to all my former writing clients from my many years as a literary agent, I love you all and forgive the ones who need forgiving.

FOREWORD

When you are standing outside of the door and looking in, Hollywood appears to be a huge, forbidding arena surrounded by enormous KEEP OUT signs that seem to be aimed at you. The odd thing is that this is far from true. Everyone is allowed in if you follow the rules, meet the criteria, and stay the course.

The hard part is that no one tells you the rules or the criteria or what the heck the course really is. Perhaps I can help. Everyone seems to think that the world of movies and television is pretty freewheeling and filled with creative types who listen to the beat of their own drummers. Not exactly true. This is a business that runs like any other business. Yes, of course it runs on the fuel of creative energy and talent, but it wouldn't run at all if it weren't for the business minds that keep everything in order.

The scary part is that the "rules" are secret. Usually you have to learn them as you go. Unfortunately if you don't learn them quickly enough, you are out before you really get in. This book is designed to give you inside knowledge of how to get into the Hollywood world, and, equally as important, how to stay in.

When I began my career as a literary agent in Hollywood I saw that there wasn't a handbook to teach me the ropes. I learned as I went along. I learned from whomever was willing to teach me and just took it on faith that they were right. There is no college course on navigating this industry. I wrote this book to make your climb easier. It will help you make decisions, choices, take the right actions, and understand what's happening while you are in the middle of the whirlwind – all of which will make show business much more fun.

I GETTING STARTED

MIND YOUR OWN BUSINESS!

I love writers. That's a fact. I always have. I've admired their tenacity, devotion to their craft, their willingness to go that extra mile for little or no reward, their single-mindedness and their wonderfully imaginative minds. I've even loved their sweetness and insecurities as well as – sometimes – their narcissism and their outrageous demands.

As an agent I spent over twenty-five years protecting them, listening to them, reading their work, and strategizing their careers. I negotiated their deals, fought with studio lawyers about their contracts, handled their money, and cared about their lives. Agents do so much more then simply submit scripts to producers.

When I left the agency business and began a new career as a writer's consultant, it hit me like a ton of bricks that new writers as well as pros knew little or nothing of how to maneuver the business of their writing careers. For many years I have been asked questions by professional writers, novices, college students, and even family and friends about the business of writing for the screen. As a writer, you need to understand the behind-the-scenes goings on of your career. You need to understand what is being said as well as what is not being said and what is simply implied in a meeting or on a phone call. You need to know who to talk to and what to say and when to stop talking. You need to know how to read the contract of your script or option deal and how the different points in it will affect you now and even years from now.

Throughout my years in the business I've learned all the "ins and outs" of a writer's business and creative life. As a consultant my work with writers includes helping them get their work into shape so that it is marketable for the Hollywood community. However, I've found that learning to master the creative aspects of writing is not enough to secure success as a writer. This is true whether your medium is motion pictures or television.

Through my tenure as an agent, I was involved in the lives of hundreds of writers, producers, directors, and the occasional actor, and I saw how little they knew about their "business." Artists may be famous for their craft, may be lauded and given awards, but can still spend years at the mercy of the system that defines them. This is neither a productive nor a safe state of being. The fact that artists often don't understand the business of their creative careers can, and often does, destroy them. As an artist, you can be led to the slaughter by well-meaning but inadequate advisors as well as mean-spirited, selfish egotists who somehow manage to gain your trust. These people are only one small part of the problem. You need to understand just how much you should believe what you read in *The Hollywood Reporter* and *Variety* and how to figure out what is really being said. You need to know if you should trust your agent, manager, lawyer, and business manager, as well as which deal is right for you and which one is wrong. The list of questions is infinite.

A writer is really a small business. The creative portion of your career has a world of its own and the business side is like a foreign country.

It has often been difficult and in some cases impossible to teach artists what they need to know to protect themselves, their work, their reputations, and their livelihoods. Most creative folks simply don't want to be bothered with this side of their lives. Watching writers make poor business decisions has brought tears to my eyes, and these bad choices have ruined their careers. Writers have jumped to the wrong agents at the wrong times, trusted their money to poor-advice-givers, gone with the wrong producers who filled their heads with compliments and lies, and not trusted good agents and sat at home with excellent screenplays because they didn't know where to go or what to do with them.

Creative people are surrounded with advisors; however, in reality, you, the artist, are the one truly in charge of your life and career. As Harry Truman said, "The buck stops here." You are ultimately responsible for the final decisions you make. Make sure that you make them with all the information at your fingertips.

While working as a literary agent I represented writers, directors, and producers in motion pictures, movies for television, television series, and books. During that time I have represented and guided the careers of writers including Larry Hertzog, Christopher Lofton, Peter Bellwood, Ronnie Christensen, Carol Mendelsohn, Randall Wallace, and many, many more. I've watched my clients make wonderful decisions and terrible decisions.

If I can share some knowledge with you now, I will be happy indeed. Someone said that "knowledge is power," and this still rings true.

> EXERCISES

1.   Call at least five well-known writers for an interview.

2.   Ask what decisions helped their careers.

3.   Ask what decisions hurt their careers.

4.   Ask about the turning point in their careers.

5.   Ask about their best and worst agent experiences.

LADIES AND GENTLEMEN, START YOUR ENGINES

2

There are many reasons people believe that they can become, or already are, writers. Sometimes their friends and/or relatives tell them that they are great storytellers. Perhaps they are avid readers, or they love movies or television. There are those who feel they have an important story to tell, and many, many people believe that writing is an easy gig that brings in lots of money.

Then there are all of those who go to the movies or watch television and say to themselves and anyone else who will listen, "I can write better than 'that'." They may write to entertain themselves and others. They write to make money, or they write because they have ideas that they feel they must share. They write to express their feelings or to hide them. The reasons go on for miles.

Whatever the impetus, the result is the same: All writers want to share their stories with others. Writers want their stories to be seen, read, or heard. Accomplishing that goal can be a great challenge. Choosing your medium is crucial. Trying to make up your mind whether to tell your story as a novel, TV sitcom, or drama, or as a screenplay, short story, poem, or a play will be one of your most important life decisions. I've often read projects that were in the wrong medium, and thus failed to see the light of day.

The expression, "Follow your gut," applies to the type of writing you choose as well as the business aspects of your creative life. With that said I must advise you to try different types of writing to find your comfort level.

Your first big surprise will be that you cannot simply sit down and write a great script. No one can and that's the truth. Believe it. I know that you want to argue with me on this, but don't. Even if you have a great story or wonderful action sequences, your first script is practice. You will need to see if you can figure out the three-act structure, and if your characters are flat or alive. You will need to learn the difference between a good plot and a humdrum one. There are a multitude of things you will need to learn about the narrative process before you begin to put words on paper.

You will need to acquire a great deal of knowledge about form and substance, and about style and imagery, before you even begin to write that first script. You will need to learn how so many things that comprise a great screenplay must fall together to make it work. You can do this by attending film school, taking individual classes and lots of writing seminars, and learning from all of those kind and patient professional writers who might be willing to spend their time with you. Film schools can give you a head start on the process, as will many writing seminars, books, and CDs. Just be sure these courses are given by people who are excellent in their fields. If you are going to use a consultant, check out his or her qualifications thoroughly. There are many great books and videos on the subject of screenwriting and even great screenwriting magazines. Read, research, and study everything you can get your hands on.

Subscribe to good writers' magazines like *Creative Screenwriting*; go to the The Writer's Store in Westwood if you are lucky enough to live in or near the Los Angeles area. Go online and get information about other magazines and writers' books. There are zillions of them. Go to every lecture and seminar that you can get to. Listen, ask questions and learn, learn, learn.

Okay, now, let's say you've decided to write a screenplay. It's time to proceed to the next step: writing your first script. This is a monumental task.

First you need to find a story that:

    a. you want to tell;

    b. has not already been told in exactly this way;

    c. has an enormous amount of people all over the world who will be interested in seeing it (not just your relatives);

    d. is a story about which you know something; and

    e. is a story that has some truth and underlying meaning to it.

Not as easy as you thought, right? Let's keep going.

Now that you have an idea (story) and some characters in your mind that will make the story work, you may begin. The process will be much slower than you thought it would be. You might find that the characters don't seem to make sense, the pacing may seem all wrong, the comedy (or drama) falls flat, and you will forget why you thought this was such a good idea in the first place. Don't let those things stop you. Writing involves a great deal of rewriting and a great deal of thought. Continue with the work until the screenplay is complete; then put it down for two weeks, pick it up, and read it straight through. Whether you hate it or think that it's the best writing in the world, now rewrite it again and then again.

After all of this time-consuming work, once you feel that you have completed this first, fabulous script, you need to acknowledge to yourself that this was just a learning process. Your first script should probably never see the light of day. You may want to have a close family member read it, but that's all, no one else. No one writes a great first script – but don't let it deter you from moving forward. If you can't follow this advice you may want to give it to a professional screenplay consultant (script doctor) who will be able to judge the work in a constructive way.

If you are serious about being a screenwriter, start your second script right away. I promise that it will be much better than the first one. As a screenplay consultant I watch my clients improve their writing with each new draft, after receiving my notes. When you are close to a project it is often difficult to see it objectively.

The most successful writer I ever represented as an agent came to me after having written eighteen original screenplays and three novels. He said, "The first eighteen were awful. I'll never show them to anyone." The screenplay that he did give me was wonderful and I sold it to Disney Studios within a month for $750,000. That was the beginning of a young writer's career that was like riding a rocket.

It may not be necessary for you to write eighteen screenplays, but my point is that it takes a lot of time, practice, and dedication to become a good writer.

I cannot explain to you about "creative juices" "writer's block" "down time," "being dry," or "being on a roll." You will feel them, or not. This is a field of dedication and self-motivation. It's up to you to sit down and do the work. There is no glamour when you are alone in a room with a computer and silence. The glamour, excitement, and big bucks come later after you have learned your craft and made that first and second sale.

You need tenacity to make it as a writer. There is no other way to become successful in this field than to hang in and continue to write and write and write.

Something must take place in your mind, heart, and brain if you are to become a great writer. You need the combination of your life experiences, daydreams, imaginings, and hopes. You will need to call upon your moments of despair and elation as well as all of the emotions you have felt throughout your life. It will help to remember the conflicts and feelings of people you know as well as your own. All of these events will give life to the characters that you create, make them real, and make them resonate with truth. Even wacky comedies and horror pictures need to have some underlying meaning to them to make them special enough to produce.

I also recommend that you get out of the house and experience life as much as possible. Travel, meet people, and see new sights and cities. Taste new foods, hear new music — use these resources for your work. The knowledge you will gain will make a tremendous difference between you and others who wish to be writers. Great scripts have honesty in their characters. The all-important character arc and the theme of your piece must speak to the human condition. This will set you apart from the average new writer.

Okay, now you've taken those classes, learned the basics, purchased the proper computer and screenplay-formatting program, and you have finished your first screenplay. It's time to look within yourself to see whether this is still the career that you choose. If it is, then it is time to go back and do it again.

When you begin your next script, you will have so much more to give it than that first one or second one. I believe that if you have chosen a genre that you love, you should write the next one in that same genre. Conversely, if that first genre wasn't a good fit, then try another. To perfect your area you need to keep going until you find it. Whatever genre you feel comfortable with is the one you need to work on again.

> EXERCISES

1. Write a one-act play.

2. Using the same plot, write it as a short story.

3. Use that idea as the basis for a screenplay.

4. Rewrite that screenplay three times.

5. Buy a book on screenwriting and read it twice.

6. Work out five to ten different story ideas for your next projects.

7. Sign up to hear a professional writer speak.

KICKIN' IT UP A NOTCH

Getting a screenplay down on paper is difficult, there's no doubt about that. Making it great is even harder. However, if you don't try you may end up living in mediocrity, and you will never get the kudos and rewards of a successful writer.

A great screenplay and film has "legs." That means that people will want to see the movie over and over again. They might want to bring their friends, or rent the film on DVD, or purchase a copy to own. A great screenplay has meaning beyond the ability to entertain. Even romantic and teen comedies can have depth and wisdom without sacrificing humor.

The secret for writing a great screenplay is not in finding the most unusual story — it is in writing up to the high standards described in the following pages.

CHARACTER ARC

No one wants to stay with a film or screenplay if the main character does not grow internally, does not learn something important about himself, and does not become a better, smarter, or more lovable person. Whether the film is *Booty Call* or *Pride and Prejudice*, you will notice the growth of the main characters and love them for it.

UNDERLYING THEME

A great movie is not about the plot. It is about what is going on beneath the surface. It is about something emotionally important or deals with a universal problem of great significance. Jim Carrey's *Mask* is about the insecurities of all people. It is about the main character's feelings of inadequacy and personal fears. You must find a way to touch something that can tap into the collective and often unconscious needs of people in general. Even the animated classic, *Bambi*, is about all of our fears of abandonment. As a writer you need to know what you are trying to say about the human condition. Without becoming preachy and pious you can impart wisdom and help people to understand themselves and others in a new and constructive way. You have the ammunition to educate as well as entertain. This will set your script apart from the masses of material that are spewed out every year. Take the time to understand your characters and know why they do what they do. The psychological aspects of a story need to be dead-on.

DIALOGUE

I heard that it was the great actress, Helen Hayes, who once said "If it aint on the page, it aint on the stage." Nothing in a screenplay is as bad as boring dialogue. You must learn to write characters who speak with unique voices. They must jump off the page with personality, wit, and exceptionally clever ways of saying things. Each character in the piece needs to have a distinct personal quality and voice.

I've always hated screenplays that make me go back and forth from where I am reading to the opening sequences that introduce the characters. If I cant remember which one is Sally and which one is Susan, you havent done your job. Find the inner core of each important character and have them speak in their own distinctive manner.

PACING

If your pacing is slow, or worse, if it is repetitive, you will lose your reader in just a few pages. Keep moving the story forward like a shark in the water, never stopping, never holding back or overanalyzing itself. If the reader's mind starts to wander at any point in your story, then you have lost a sale. If you spend too much time describing where people are or what they are wearing or the weather, you will lose your pace. Let the characters maintain the pace through their interaction with one another.

LIKABILITY OF THE MAIN CHARACTERS

If readers care about the people in the story, they will want to go forward with the script. Likability is more difficult to explain than it appears on its face. Sean Penn's character in the 1996 film, *Dead Man Walking*, is an obnoxious murderer. By the end of the movie, the audience understands him and has some sympathy for the child he once was and the unhappy adult he became. Of course our real sympathy goes out to Sister Prejean, played by the great Susan Sarandon. There must be someone to root for in a film — a character whom the audience sides with, and in whose future the audience invests. This character need not be the lead. It may be a juicy character role — the protagonist's parent or even grandparent, for example. Anyone in the screenplay will do, as long as we care about someone.

● ● ●

Certainly there are more facets to a good screenplay than those I've just introduced, and those you will learn in film schools and books. The professional-looking format and the short exposition matter quite a bit. However, if you want to raise the standard of excellence in your writing, I suggest you concentrate heavily on seeing if the five points above are well covered in your next project. Go the extra mile. These five points will separate you from the crowd, and will turn a comedy, thriller, drama, family film, or love story into a great screenplay.

> EXERCISES

1. Write a history of each main character in your story or screenplay.

2. Write a description of the psychological makeup for each of these characters.

3. Review your story to see what you really want to tell the world.

4. Write what it is that your main character needs to overcome and how you will resolve his or her dilemma.

NO ONE TO BLAME BUT YOURSELF

To have a successful career, a writer must make many decisions that have nothing to do with the act of setting down words on paper. These decisions have harmed and even destroyed the careers of some of the most accomplished talents. The potential problems may arise without your seeing them as problems at all, but if you make the wrong choice it may be catastrophic. I will try to help you avoid some of the major issues that you will face.

Writers are terribly insecure when they put that first toe in the water. They often feel that it might be easier if they had a partner. You may think that by having a partner you will avoid dry spells, because when you are out of ideas, your partner will come up with some. You may hate the idea of sitting all alone every day and starring at that blank computer screen. Of course we have all heard the old adage that "two heads are better than one." Well, think again.

As an agent I always preferred writers who work solo. Early on in my career I learned that partnerships inevitably break up and it was usually impossible to get an assignment for one-half of a team, whether they were well-known or not.

If you decide you really must work in a partnership, the best situation would be finding someone with similar likes and dislikes — someone with whom you can spend many, many hours within a closed room. It would also be better if you both smoked or hated smoking, if you both liked working all night or were both morning people. It would be great if at least one of you could make great coffee or repair a computer. Many things one needs from a partner seem inconsequential at first, but may become enormous issues after a few months. Sounds like a marriage, and in many ways it is.

You also need someone with at least a modicum of discipline and who is in it with you for the long haul. This last point is crucial. During my agency tenure I represented a fairly successful comedy writing team of two middle-aged women. They were smart, funny, and actively involved in their sitcom-writing career. They were both married. One writer had been a comic actress and was married to a comedian. One was a little ditzy, the other was more grounded. They balanced each other quite well. I'll call them Mitzi and Fritzi. I loved them and was thrilled to be their agent. They had been together for a while but eventually things began to break down between them. Just when I thought we were about to break through and get them a staff job for a sitcom, they broke up their partnership. It destroyed both of their writing careers. No one, not even I, could tell whether it was Mitzi or Fritzi who had more of the writing chops. Neither of them would write spec scripts. They felt it was beneath them and that their "credits" were enough. Once a team is established, they are not trusted by anyone to write separately. I was so sorry to see them go as clients. They never worked much as writers again.

The breakup of writing partnerships happens more often than not. It is, without a doubt, devastating to the careers of both writers. Let me reiterate that if you can write alone, please do so.

At some point during your pursuit of a career, another writer may ask you to partner up on a project. The final product will never be a good writing sample for you because no one will know which one of you did most of the creative work. Writing samples are paramount to your writing career. You need as many of them as possible, and all of them should be original scripts that have been written by you alone.

Recently I was a guest speaker at a writers' conference and had a private consultation with an interesting woman. Here was her conundrum: She was just starting a screenwriting career and felt that since she was middle-aged and female that it would be impossible for her to be accepted into the male and obsessively youth-oriented "biz." She had decided to put her adult son's name on her screenplays as either the writer or perhaps her co-writer. She suggested that if her scripts garnered any interest and generated any meetings, he would go to them alone. She asked my advice about this situation. I was appalled.

My chief horror was that it was a lie. Lying in any business or in any facet of one's life is always a poor choice. This terrible subterfuge cannot continue in a writer's career. Suppose she was to have a meeting. How would her son be able to talk intelligently about the project, or pitch her other ideas, or come up with ways of making the script better? How would he be able to answer on-the-spot questions about the characters of "his" writing process? All in all, it just wouldn't work. I explained to her that when it comes to original screenplays, no one cares how old you are or which sex you are or if you are a green elf. It is all about the script itself. If it is great it will sell. You will probably be re-written no matter who you are. Be proud of having done a great job. Be proud of who you are. Writing samples are usually sent out prior to a meeting so the reader doesn't know anything about the writer personally. The written word speaks for itself. If you have the talent, people will want you and your work. I've found that your attitude is more important than your age or sex. If you are older than everyone else in the meeting and you have a condescending or patronizing attitude toward these younger people, you will not be welcomed back. I know it's difficult to listen to advice from people younger than you are, but that's the name of the game.

If you have a good sense of humor and a positive attitude you will be accepted. It's up to you.

Here is another issue that I've known to be a hard choice for writers. Currently, novel agents and novel publishers want books that can be sold later as motion pictures. It is a very high priority in this field. Opting for whichever medium suits you and your story idea is completely your choice. This is a question of following your heart or perhaps following the momentary fad of the business. If you write purely for a sale, and out of panic, there will be a hole in the work that the reader can detect either consciously or unconsciously, and your reputation will be hurt. You simply cannot please everyone. Writing is difficult at best, but when it is forced into a genre that you don't love, your writing will suffer. When writing from your heart you may not sell the work but you will have a wonderful writing sample. This will eventually do more good for you than you can imagine.

The harsh rules of business have intruded irrevocably on your esthetic world. Not only must books be movies, but movie producers and studios want to sell their soundtracks and turn their movies into video games, DVD sales, board games, and toys because the "backend" monies can be huge to a studio. Motion picture financiers want big movies based on comic books, so people are trying to get comic books published before they think they can sell their scripts.

No matter what changes occur in our business, the same rule will always apply to writers working on spec screenplays: Write that project in which you believe.

The movie business has become so complex that it may seem impossible to navigate it in terms of knowing whom you want to please. My experience tells me that writers should always please themselves first and foremost but to always keep the market in mind. I know that sounds contradictory; however, it's possible and it works. The quality of your work will rise along with your passion for your project. When you write only because you want to get a sale, it will show in the work. Everyone in town is always searching for that special writer with that special spec script that rarely comes along. Very often, your script may not sell or even be optioned; however, you may be hired for a different project and you will use those skills that shone in your original screenplay to rewrite someone else's film. Your spec script may be ahead of its time, or perhaps other screenplays with the same or similar themes are already being developed at a movie studio. I can't tell you how many times this has occurred while I was an agent — sometimes an idea is in the air and is being developed in more than one place. If you have a great script, it will serve to open many doors for you, whether it is sold or not. If the story is wonderful and the characters even better, people in the film industry will know it and will find you. The people who are making movies often find a novel, short story, news article, etc., that they will need to have a good writer translate into a movie script. Perhaps you will be the writer they hire to write that movie.

There is an old saying that "rules are made to be broken." I believe that to be true. So, if you hear that no one is buying unpackaged spec scripts, or that only books that can be movies will be published, or that you must only write big action-adventure flicks, even though you love writing relationship dramas, you are being sorely misinformed. The only real reality is that things change. The pendulum is constantly swinging back and forth. When you are absolutely sure that no one will buy and produce a western, someone remakes the very old movie, *3:10 to Yuma*, starring Russell Crowe. I don't suggest you fight only uphill battles. Try to be circumspect in your choices.

A big no-no is to spend your time and creative energy writing the same project in more than one medium. I've seen people write the same story in different mediums thinking that they will then have a better chance at a sale. It is much better to write each story idea in one format that you really love. When you do so you will write with more quality and it will show in your piece. You must always be moving forward to your next beloved project. I knew a successful writer who became too attached to one idea. He wrote his "story" as a screenplay and a novel and when they didn't sell, he also wrote it as a play. All of these efforts took their toll in time, thought, energy, and work. It was an enormous waste of all of that and it ended his career.

The simple answer is and always has been: Write what you love but remember that you are in the business of writing.

Another huge question that arises is when to let go of a script that hasn't sold. Writers quite often continually push their agents to send out an old script. It is great to believe in your work; however, here again you must trust your agent or manager. It is very hard to define why a good script doesn't sell, but usually there is a reason. You and your agent may never figure it out. It will also be possible that your agent will know, but not want to share, this information with you. Perhaps your agent feels it will hurt your feelings or that you are so tied to the project that you won't listen to the advice presented to you. The point is to simply let it go and move on to your next spec script, treatment, or pitch idea. There is no such thing as successfully selling defensively. If you force your agent's hand he or she will be put in a position of having to go against his or her own instincts or to let you go as a client. Either of these decisions are potential disasters for you. Like the old saying goes, "It doesn't matter if the window hits the rock or the rock hits the window, in either case it's bad for the window."

Similarly there is a huge problem if you write a script that your agent doesn't believe in and doesn't want to submit. This is a dead zone that can destroy a perfectly good agent–client relationship. It has happened to me. I once represented a brilliant writer who blindsided me by walking into my office with twenty gold-stamped, leather-bound, completed screenplays about the murders of elderly people in an old age home. A script doesn't get more depressing than that. The story was so sad that I could barely read it. There were no young heroes nor were there any of the other elements that are so necessary in a commercial script. I was dumbfounded that he had written this without discussing it with me first and that he had brought it in to me in a condition that practically screamed that he would not do any rewriting. It was the end of our professional relationship and I'm sorry to say that his career never took off.

There are so many sticky situations that arise in your decision-making process. Arguing vociferously with your producer or development executive in a notes meeting is another one. You can only go so far defending your creative choices. Once a deal has been made, once you are writing on someone else's dime, they have the final say, even if it's wrong. Certainly you may present your case and even try to find a middle ground, but the person behind the desk is the one in power. If you begin by making enemies, you will be replaced on your own film and get a terrible reputation in this very small town.

There's no such thing as "common sense" when it comes to navigating a career in Hollywood. It's better to discuss your situation or problem with someone who has some experience in your field. If possible you must find mentors and ask their advice. People love to give advice. Just be careful to ask a pro.

Another big decision is when to write another spec script. Perhaps your career has been going along fairly well. You have a pretty good agent and you have optioned a couple of scripts and had the good fortune of being paid for a couple of rewrites on other people's scripts. You may have met with lots of good development people and some fine producers, maybe even a studio executive or two. Then, one day it dawns on you that it has been awfully quiet for a few months. Nothing is happening. You call your agent and ask the inevitable questions: "What's going on? Can't you get me another assignment? Is anything happening on my old scripts?" Obviously the answer to all of the above is a resounding "No." Your agent asks, "What are you working on now?" He wants to know if you have any new pitches. You realize that you have been waiting for him to find you the next job. It's easier to blame your agent than to take responsibility for your own inaction. As I've mentioned previously you must always be working on a new spec script. This means at any time in your career. When the going gets tough you better get yourself to your computer. I once worked for a wonderful agent named Mel Bloom. When told by a client that he'd already paid his dues, Mel replied, "Have you paid them this year?"

All of the above are potentially serious problems in a writer's life. Pay attention to the big picture of your career. Be sensible and sensitive to the business you are in. Certainly there are more problem areas than these, but these are amazingly common and have destroyed many writers. Try to weigh your decisions carefully, and be open to listening to folks who have been swimming in these waters before you. We can't avoid making mistakes in this life; however, perhaps you will be able to sidestep a few.

WHAT'S HOT AND WHAT'S NOT

Every agent in town is waiting for you to bring them the next big saleable screenplay that will knock the business off its axis. They want you to bring them that piece that will have producers and studios panting at their doors with their tongues hanging out and with huge offers of money and multiple deals for future movie writing assignments. Agents want the best for you, because it means the best for them. I happen to believe that the agent-writer relationship is a great one. It is an honest quid pro quo — if you are successful... I am successful. How bad is that?

Okay, so how do you make that happen? How do you deliver a perfectly written project that will make the town sit up and take notice? It's not as difficult as it sounds. The first thing you have to do is to stop thinking that you must write the most unusual script of all time. This kind of thinking will destroy your chances of not only selling the script, but of keeping your agent. Yes, you search endlessly for that "different" story, for that unusual and fantastic arena that you are sure no one else has done or will do. I've found that new writers often have the tendency to try to impress people by "thinking outside the box." Well folks, the "box" is there for a reason — it works. Stay grounded in reality and tell a good and entertaining story, in an established genre, that has some believability. Throughout movie history, audiences have loved certain types of films. They go to see them over and over again. Certain genres, such as thrillers, love stories, adventures, and great dramas are evergreen; they are the fodder we live on. When you are working to get into the business, go with the flow. Perhaps, after you've established yourself as a player, you might be able to expand your horizons, but it's not the way to get into the mainstream of your chosen field.

Insofar as your early spec scripts are concerned, here are eleven rules to live by:

1. NO TOGAS ALLOWED

By this I'm referring to period pieces. Keep your early scripts contemporary. Period pieces are extremely difficult to sell. They go in and out of favor with the studios by the minute. You never know whether you are too early or too late with your piece. You may want to write a great western but very few are developed and produced. I loved *Gladiator* as well as *3:10 to Yuma*, both of which starred Russell Crowe, and naturally I love all films based on Jane Austen's novels, but movies centered in these eras are few and far between. They are not good as writing samples since they are too dependent on very specific eras. This means manners, customs, morals, societal relationships, styles of speech, costumes, etc. Period pieces are also extremely expensive to produce.

2. KEEP IT SIMPLE

Stay away from twins. Don't make a script too complicated to produce. As soon as a development executive or producer sees this he or she will toss it into the "circular file." It is too much of a pain in the neck. Try not to write a script that is so complicated that it would make the casting a horror or the locations (see #4 on page 25) impossible to get to. Another example (besides twins) is a multigenerational story involving a large and diverse cast. This means a nightmare of casting as well as costume and set changes that are a financial pain. Don't go there. Besides, no one really wants to watch a bunch of people age before his or her eyes. Of course the antithesis of this statement would be that wonderful movie, *Cocoon*, where the older people became young and there were young stars in it. That film caught the imagination of its audience in a very favorable way. After all, who doesn't want to stay alive and youthful forever?

3. KEEP 'EM YOUNG

If you really want to kick-start your writing career, try to have your early scripts feature a fairly young cast. In my mind the term "young" means up to twenty-nine years old. Not one minute older. Even in *The Curious Case of Benjamin Button*, the main character grew younger.

The youth market is what is most viable today. Actually if you can write a script for nine-to-twelve-year-old boys and their young parents, you are really in good shape. The research shows that this demographic will return to see the same film over and over again, with different friends and family members. Recidivism is the word. Let's not forget our little friends *Harry Potter*, *Wolverine*, *Spider-Man*, and *Superman*, ad infinitum.

4. LOCATION, LOCATION, AND LOCATION

This is not simply a rule in real estate. This is a real consideration in movie-making. A studio never has a problem putting its money in a viable movie star who can "open" a movie. Opening a movie means a guarantee of big bucks at the box office in the film's opening weekend. Foreign or multiple locations do not promise this type of income for the film and they are very expensive. You don't *have to* keep everything set in one city, but you should remember that this option could be an attractive one to those who might purchase your screenplay. You always want to be realistic in your writing. Think bottom line about locations but think expensive with starring roles and action sequences.

5. THE STAR

Here are the rules for your main character and they are hard and fast. These points apply to all genres. Do not try to change them for any reason.

a. The Star's character is on every page.

b. The Star's character resolves the problem.

c. The Star's character has the most lines.

d. The Star's character gets the girl (or the guy).

e. The Star's character is the smartest person in the cast.

f. The Star's character has the last word in the film.

g. The Star's character must grow as a person.

h. The Star's character must learn something about
him- or herself.

It seems that many fine actors and stars are drawn to political thrillers. These can be great spec scripts. They show the writer's abilities with intricate plots and great characters. Think George Clooney in *Michael Clayton*, *The Good German*, and *Syriana*.

6. COINCIDENCES

They can only be used to complicate the plot. Coincidences and coincidental accidents should never resolve the problems. When you use this device to solve an important plot point the audience feels cheated.

7. GLOOMY VERSUS DRAMAS

There is a fine line between being depressing and being dramatic. You need to learn the difference between them while you are in the early stages of your dramatic writing career. I love a good dramatic relationship film. I hate depressing movies that have no other saving grace but to be sad. *Hud* was a great drama starring the late Paul Newman and Patricia Neal. Another golden oldie was the 1957 film, *A Face in the Crowd*, starring Patricia Neal and Andy Griffith. The more recent film, *Revolutionary Road*, with Leonardo DiCaprio and Kate Winslet, is another example of a terrific drama where the audience really is entertained while learning a great deal about honesty and relationships. A good drama has the ability to teach the audience some of the important truths in our lives. They often deal with right and wrong, good and bad, and many of the moral decisions each of us is faced with during our stay on this planet. These are films that must be seen and studied by serious film writers. They define great drama with riveting characters whom the audience wants to stay with. The audience becomes invested in their lives and we learn something about the human condition. *Hud* speaks to survival and inner strength while

A Face in the Crowd tells us that total power corrupts totally when there is inner weakness. There is a difference between depressing and drama. Always keep in mind that you are in the business of entertainment.

8. CHOICES

Whether you write a contemporary drama, comedy, suspense, thriller, murder-mystery, teen comedy, or romance, you must keep your characters interesting and believable. You need the audience to become involved with what happens to them. The great writers know that it is the characters whom the audiences fall in love with, and that what the characters do and say in movies are what keeps those audiences coming back. Try to write "up" to the audience's intellect and emotions. We want to leave the movie theater feeling like we were entertained and that we learned just a little bit about the human condition. The movie studios like this too.

9. PERSONALITY

Whether you are writing a huge action picture or small romantic comedy or teen coming-of-age story, it is all about those main characters. An audience must love someone in any movie. They need to root for someone and to care what happens to them. Audiences automatically like Tom Hanks, but you may not get him so you must write a great character that would work for any actor who ends up starring in your movie. We all always hope that wonderful, talented actors will be cast in pictures, but we also know how rarely that happens. Lately, there seem to be more celebrities in films than serious actors.

10. DON'T GO TOO CRAZY

Oh, and by the way, try to stay on this planet. By this I mean in our realm of reality, within the scope of reason. Every time I start to read a script that takes place inside someone's brain or has some mystical fervor, or where a person morphs into another entity, my mind starts to wander. Writers often try to find and create unique situations that are so far out that they bear little or no resemblance to real life or real people. Trying to be unusual can be a trap for new writers as well as established pros. I love science-fiction films but even they need one foot in the real world of people and relationships. Studios also don't like to make fools of our American heroes. We can't sell Adam Sandler portraying George Washington for laughs or a musical comedy set in the Alamo. There seems to be some sort of taboo about it. Go figure.

11. BUDGETS

It has been interesting to me to note that, particularly when it comes to thrillers, writers often think in terms of low-budget films. I have found that one of the biggest disparities between low- and high-budget thrillers is often simply the casting. Why not think in terms of a high budget when you first enter the game with a new screenplay? If that doesn't pan out you can always try the lower budget, independent market later.

What I am trying to tell you is to play it straight. It doesn't matter if it's a comedy, tragedy, drama, or action film — keep your characters and stories honest and true to themselves. For new writers trying to get into the mainstream of Hollywood it is best to keep these rules in mind. You will always find exceptions to these rules but don't let that fool you. Start out with a good, simple story and hone your craft. Remember why you want to tell a particular story. Does your movie inspire, entertain, and teach a life lesson? These points are not easy to accomplish, but they are always in style at the studios and the box office.

● ● ●

> EXERCISES

1.   Reread your own screenplays.

2.   Change anything that doesn't coincide with the above information.

3.   See if you can simplify your plot and complicate your characters.

4.   Check the "calendar" section of your Sunday newspaper every week to see what the studios and production companies are making.

5.   Keep a list of these films for future reference.

MIRROR, MIRROR ON THE WALL

6

Presenting yourself seems simple enough. You simply show up. Are there right and wrong ways to present yourself? You bet. I'm sure you think that you are cool, hip, and with it. You think you know how to dress yourself properly and in an acceptable manner, especially since this is show biz and you've heard that anything goes. You believe that since you are a "creative type," most standard value systems don't count for you. You think of yourself as an artist who can do things your own way. *Not!*

It's not just the way you dress; be aware of the many elements that are very important in how you present yourself. Hopefully you will be meeting with important people who will have a profound effect on your business and creative life. These people need to be comfortable with you and they need to believe that you are dependable and trustworthy. Remember that in a sense you are asking them to spend millions of dollars on you and your work. This is a tremendous responsibility for you and for them. These are very busy people with many others vying for their time. If and when you finally get that chance to meet with them, you don't want to blow it over some minor infraction that you don't even realize you committed, such as wearing flip-flops.

You may be a writer, but you are looking for a writing career. The career part is what you may be playing fast and loose with by way of your personal presentation. Remember grammar school? Neatness still counts and so do a lot of other things that may have slipped your mind since childhood.

Here are ten do's and don'ts, based on my years watching clients destroy themselves in ways that had absolutely nothing to do with their writing talent and ability:

1. DRESSING WELL

You have a meeting at a studio or production company, or you have signed up for a "pitch" session. You are going anywhere where you might meet someone who is connected in any way with the entertainment business. You are going to hear a speaker at a writer's seminar or to meet with a possible agent or manager. It's jeans, right? Okay, but what about that T-shirt? Wrong. What about shorts, baggy or otherwise? Wrong. What about high heels and a tiny, tiny skirt? Wrong.

First of all everything needs to be clean. That includes your shoes, pants, tops, purses, hair, skin, and fingernails. The jeans are fine if worn with a sport shirt (preferably with long sleeves, rolled up) or a collared knit shirt. With regard to women, the same principles apply vis a vis the jeans and a nice blouse or shirt. The people you are meeting will notice if you are a mess or unkempt. You want them to notice your work and ideas, not your dirty fingernails or great legs. You don't want to overdress in a suit and tie, and you may not want to dress in the long-skirt-and-turquoise-jewelry look or as the "artiste," since these outfits may be more dominant than your screenplay ideas.

Try to keep your wardrobe simple. Let the people you are meeting see *you*, not your outfit. Let them hear what you have to say, not focus on your costume.

I once represented a writer who co-wrote a spec comedy, which sold for $850,000 and was produced and released very quickly. It was a hit and the writers were wooed all over town. They had decided to write separately after that script, but since my client had been a TV comedy writer, most production companies wanted to see him right away. I set up meeting after meeting for him. Some of the companies that wanted to meet with him had mentioned that they had open writing assignments they thought he could fill. As time went by and nothing came of these meetings, I finally asked him to stop by after one of them. He walked into my office and I was appalled by his appearance. He was a big, muscular man who was wearing hiking shorts, a skimpy tank top, and hiking books. He looked like an ad for some macho man magazine. (I'd only met with this writer a couple of times and he was always dressed in a casual, but respectful manner.) Then he sat down and didn't stop talking for twenty minutes straight. That's how I found out why he would never work again and he never did.

2. ARRIVALS

If you are on time, then you are late. Get to your meeting-place a little early. Remember you have to find a parking place, find the right office or building or restaurant, and most important, you do not want to keep your meeting waiting. If you are ten minutes late they will hate you, if you are fifteen minutes late they will probably not see you. The people you will meet are extremely busy or like to think that they are and want *you* to think that they are. You are the low man on this totem pole so you must arrive early. It shows you respect their superior position. If there is some emergency that keeps you from being early, you must call their office and explain and ask if you can be late or if you should re-schedule, as you apologize profusely. It better be a damn good reason. Early on in my agency career I was Larry Hertzog's first agent. Larry was always early to a meeting, admitting that if "one isn't early, then one is late." Larry became a most successful television writer, executive producer, and series creator. He created *Tin Man* and *Nowhere Man*, and wrote and produced many shows for Stephen J. Cannell Productions as well as others. Even after all of his success, he was still early to meetings. Larry once told me that he always sort of "skulked" around outside of my office suite, until it was time for our meeting. I found that to be very endearing.

3. DEPARTURES

This one is hard to quantify but I'll try. Don't overstay your welcome. Be sensitive to body language, roving eyes, clock-checking, and taking calls. These are sure signs that the meeting is over. Once you've been served your coffee or fancy water, had a five-to-ten minute social chit-chat session, pitched your project or yourself, and heard what the other guy has to say, the meeting is usually over. Most meetings don't go over thirty to forty-five minutes. Once you see them start to shove their chairs back, you must stand up and begin to thank them for their time and interest, then leave. Don't hang around with long good-byes. These are painful to busy people and may cost you dearly.

No one wants to work with a pain in the ass and if you can't end a meeting they won't give you the writing assignment.

4. TALKING

Not as easy as it seems. Aside from pitching your project, you must do some P.R. on yourself. That means sharing. Not a dirty word, guys. If you don't talk a little about yourself, they will never remember you. Keep this part of the meeting short, but it is important. I can't stress this enough. You want to be remembered. These people hear movie stories every day, over and over again. It's nice for them to hear a little about a real person that they meet. There may be more than one person in your meeting. Quite often producers or agents will have development executives or assistants in the room with you. Try to keep as much of your conversation toward the main power in the room. Don't be pulled into talking too much to anyone else. Without being rude, return your attention to the person behind the desk.

5. LISTENING

I've represented more than one compulsive talker in my life and they rarely got the job. If you talk too much, you'll be out on your ass and never seen again. Listen to what is being said by others. Ask questions, and show interest in the answers.

6. ENTHUSIASM

Above all, be enthusiastic. No drooping face, foot shuffling, or moody attitudes. If you are terribly shy, get over it; you're an adult, so act like it. Firm handshake, eye-to-eye contact and a big smile are all required. Show that you're happy to be there and they will react in kind.

You have to let people believe that you believe in yourself and in your work. You must project self-confidence in your screenplays. I never want to read a script by someone who tells me that it is okay. I want someone to tell me that the script I am about to receive is great.

7. HAVE THE GOODS

If you are pitching a project, you better have the finished script or at least a well-thought-out and fairly extensive treatment to leave behind. It's even better if you have a copy of the script with you. Don't waste people's time pitching an idea if you are a new writer and don't have the pages to back it up. It's okay for the pros, but not for you. If you have pitched your finished screenplay and it is not something that the company is interested in reading, they might ask if you have any other ideas. If that happens you may pitch a few, maybe three, projects that are in various stages of development. Make it clear that these are not-yet-completed projects.

8. THE WRITTEN WORD

Show the same respect for your written work that you show for your wardrobe. Keep it clean. *No typos. No grammatical errors.* Take the time and make the effort to see that your script is perfect. As a matter of fact this applies to all of your writing, even if it's an email, letter, or invitation. Maybe you need to have it read by someone else, preferably someone very smart. Make sure the screenplay you submit has a cover page with the script title, your name, and your contact number and/or email address on it. The pages of the screenplay must be numbered, and use the thick brads with washers. A script cover is not necessary.

9. FOLLOW UP

Send a thank you note via mail or email for any kindness that was shown to you. Don't call unless that was agreed upon for a reason. Keep the note simple and direct. Thank people for speaking at an event, for hearing your pitch, for meeting with you, for giving you advice, for coming to your workshop, etc. This will remind those important connections that they were appreciated and it will keep you in their minds with a positive reaction so that when you contact them again, they will remember you kindly.

10. RESPECT

Don't take crap from anyone… except the head of a major studio. If your meeting keeps you waiting for over thirty minutes, politely tell the assistant that you have another appointment, that you will be happy to call to reschedule, and then leave. Be aware that these people will probably keep you waiting an indeterminate amount of time. Being rude is another way they like to show their power. There are a lot of stupid power plays in any field of business. The entertainment field is no different. If you wait for an hour or more, they will always treat you badly because they will know that they can. If you leave, they will remember and respect you.

In the 1980s I worked for a company known as Bloom, Levy, Schorr & Associates, a wonderful literary agency in Beverly Hills. I had set up a meeting with Zev Braun, an important producer of motion pictures and television, at his Beverly Hills office. At that time I was a middle-of-the-road type of agent who was still establishing myself in the Hollywood community. I left my office, which was not far from his, but did not give myself sufficient time to deal with the headache of finding a place to park in the heart of Beverly Hills. The street congestion was terrible and I arrived at the Zev Braun offices about seven minutes late for the appointment. The assistant buzzed Zev and let him know that I was there. I sat and waited, and waited, and waited. Zev's office was close by and I could hear him talking on the phone. His conversation was about his attempt at quitting smoking. After forty minutes of sitting there, I arose, told the assistant that I had to leave, and left. About ten minutes after I returned to my office (in a very bad mood) a call came in for me from Zev. He apologized for keeping me waiting, but he then commented that I was also responsible because I was also late. We forgave each other and laughed. Zev and I have maintained a fine working relationship ever since that fateful day.

If they continue to take long phone calls during your meeting, stand up and say that this must not be a good time and that you will call for another appointment. Then leave. If you don't show respect for yourself, they won't either. If you do show self-respect, they certainly will remember you.

> EXERCISES

1. Go over all of your screenplays and treatments very carefully to check for errors.

2. Go through your closet to make sure you always have an appropriate outfit for a meeting that is ready at a moment's notice.

3. Prior to any event or meeting, map out your route.

4. Send a thank-you note after every meeting.

5. Write a three-page treatment based on each of your projects.

TO REWRITE OR NOT TO REWRITE

Choosing a career as a writer is easy. Writing is hard. Rewriting is even harder.

As a screenplay and novel consultant I read the client's work, make correction notes on the manuscript, and do a write-up on the project's problems.

After that I have a phone conference with the writer and go over all of the notes verbally, answer any questions the writer may have, and give advice and direction regarding the business of writing and the entertainment industry.

When I was an agent I did the same thing with my writers' new screenplays. There were always notes from me about how they could and should improve their work.

Invariably the clients ask the question, "Should I rewrite this script or move on to something else?"

Writing is a very personal occupation. It's about the creative genie inside of you. It's about your ego and desires. Where are the hard and fast rules that apply to everything else? They simply don't often apply to creative writing because, for the most part, you are your own boss and that gives you the freedom of choice.

To rewrite or not to rewrite, that is the question you ask of me. I don't have a stake in this process nor does anyone in your writers' group or anyone else that you might go to for input. This baby is yours and you are asking a question for which you already know the answer.

Of course you should rewrite the script. But, having seen and listened to people's notes, you wonder if it will take too long. You wonder if you are up to the task. You wonder if this script is the right one on which to devote so much time and energy. You wonder and you wonder. Then, hopefully, you realize that rewrting is a lot of work and you are just putting off the inevitable.

Writing is a process. Rewriting is a huge part of that process. By the time you give your manuscript to someone you have rewritten it a zillion times. You might think that you're burnt out on this project or that my notes are too hard to do. If you feel this way then you need to find a different vocation. Give up the writing and go into selling printing supplies, or go back to being a lawyer or teacher or wrestler.

When you receive rewrite notes from me or anyone else it is your obligation to yourself to push a little harder and spend a little more time to improve your work. This is only the beginning. If you are able to make the jump into professional writing, you will be given more rewrite notes by producers, story editors, development executives, agents, managers, and actors. The powers that be in the business will have you rewriting yourself to death. Or, if you're really lucky, you'll be rewriting someone else, for a huge amount of money.

Do it and get used to doing it. Even if you never sell this particular piece, I guarantee that you will grow from the experience and it will add to your writing skills tremendously. It is a fabulous learning process that will help you immeasurably.

Paul Chitlik has written a wonderful book, *Rewrite*, which will be of great assistance to you. It is published by Michael Wiese Productions. Go to *www.mwp.com* to order this book.

> EXERCISES

1.   Wait two weeks after you've finished your screenplay.

2.   Read it through in one sitting.

3.   Think of how it could be better.

4.   Begin to rewrite it.

5.   Repeat exercises 1-4 above.

BEWARE OF THE PITFALLS

8

Okay now, let's assume you know that most agents work very hard to guide and nurture a writer's career. They help them with their material, they set up important meetings for clients, and they see that the right people read their material. They negotiate their deals, they share information with their clients, and they even listen to their personal problems. Is that enough? They also show an interest in their spouses and children, they try not to hurt their client's feelings when their work is rejected, they are loyal and often very caring. Agents keep their eye on the ball and an ear to the ground. They know what's going on in the business and who's buying what. Is *that* enough? Not so fast… they must let the writers go out into the world by themselves and pray that they do not do themselves harm. This is the most daunting of an agent's tasks.

Here are ten things that writers must not do:

1. DON'T GET STUCK ON ONE IDEA

I've had clients who have written the same basic story in novel, screenplay, and theatrical play form. This is an incredibly huge waste of time. An idea, no matter how much you love it, may not be saleable as a book or film or play. If you keep writing one concept then you are standing still and not moving forward in your career. I've represented writers who have wasted years on one idea. You must move on to the next project idea no matter how difficult that may be. However, if you've written a novel, whether it gets published or not, it can be considered as a movie by the motion picture or TV movie community. They will know if it has film potential. If you've written a screenplay and it doesn't garner any excitement in the film world, then you will probably not sell the concept as a novel.

2. DON'T THINK EVERYONE IS WRONG, EXCEPT YOU

When fifteen or twenty companies have turned down your project, chances are it won't sell. This can happen with a pitch, or a completed novel or screenplay. Right or wrong, they aren't buying it and there's nothing you or your agent can do about it. All an agent can do is put it "out there." If you find yourself arguing over every suggestion made by pros who want to help improve your material then the problem is probably you… not them. Yes, of course others can be wrong, but try to listen and see if there is something to their point of view. You will often meet with people who are much younger than you and you will automatically think that you know better than they do. This may not be true. Lots of young people have important jobs in the entertainment field and have grown up in it or worked hard at getting to those positions. They are often extremely bright and ambitious and are in touch with what's happening right now in the world. Listen to them.

3. DON'T RUIN A MEETING

Meetings are crucial to having a successful career in any arena. These are the people who may someday hire you, sign you, or introduce you to someone important. Take these meetings seriously. If you screw up, these people will not want to see you again. You must be totally tuned in to what is being said, who sits at the head of the table or behind the desk and most important, know what they really want from you. Not everyone has the gift of gab. Many folks are shy and uncomfortable in new or pressured surroundings. You must learn to get past these issues. See a shrink or talk to your friends or family, but one way or another you are in charge of yourself and you must overcome this problem. Try to remember when you sit in those meetings that almost everyone has some insecurity and that whomever you are meeting with needs something that you might have. Ask yourself the following questions: (a) Are you talking too much or not enough?

(b) Are you listening to the principal person in the room? (c) Did you arrive late? (d) Are you dressed appropriately? (e) Are you too argumentative? (f) Did you overstay your welcome? (g) Are you flirting inappropriately? The aforementioned are deathtraps that you have to avoid. Remember Larry Hertzog, who felt that if he wasn't thirty minutes early… then he was late? Not a bad way to think. You also need to assert your own personality and ideas into every encounter. If you don't talk and share something about yourself, they won't remember you.

4. DON'T MISS YOUR BIG CHANCE

Pay close attention to all situations that might present themselves to you. Recognize opportunities and don't be afraid to reach out and grab them — they may not come again. Often writers feel that they aren't ready for a meeting or their material isn't perfect enough to be shown to professionals. Naturally it's good to be cautious; however, do your due diligence to find out if the material is ready and then push ahead and show it. Take the project(s) to a writers' group, hire a script consultant and/or give it to a writing professional. Find out if it's as good as you hope it is. I've represented many writers who really wanted to direct. One of those clients became a producer and writer on various TV series over the years. I kept telling him to direct some episodes, but he said that he was too busy. He never fulfilled his dream to become a director.

5. DON'T CALL YOUR AGENT TOO OFTEN OR NOT OFTEN ENOUGH

If you don't seem interested in your career, why should your agent be? If you are calling every day without new material or ideas, you are nagging. Big no-no. It is the client's job to call the agent. You should check in periodically to see if they have any ideas or advice for you. Let them know that you are still out there working on new ideas and scripts. Give them an approximate time to expect this piece from you. Throw out new ideas to them for their opinion. Keep good communications going with your representatives — it will serve you well.

6. SHOW APPRECIATION TO YOUR AGENT, MANAGER, AND LAWYER

Yes, we all get paid, but sometimes that isn't enough. Everyone likes to be supported and praised. We all want someone to simply thank us for a job well done. Take them to lunch and/or buy them a simple birthday or Christmas gift. Say "thanks." This kind of positive input is also good with development executives or anyone who has gone out of his or her way for you.

7. DON'T MAKE A HABIT OF CHANGING AGENTS

Most of the time when clients change agents it's because they aren't getting work or selling their material. Is that really your agent's fault or are you not doing your job very well? Have you brought in new ideas and scripts? Are you keeping up relationships with people you've met via your agent? Are you doing everything you can to further your own career? Don't move from a small agency to a very big one. Bad idea. If a small agency has worked hard to build your career, you can bet a larger one will come along and make tremendous promises to lure you over to their client list. Invariably, you will be ignored, forgotten, mistreated, and overlooked. The big agencies will rarely give a new writer the time of day. They are in the business of making huge deals, packaging movies and television, and promoting their stars. They don't have the time or inclination to nurture new talent. Small agencies will be more likely to take a chance on an unknown writer. They usually can't compete with those big guys by taking you out to the hottest restaurants in town, or meeting you in a huge boardroom filled with other impressive-looking agents in their Armani suits. The small, "boutique" agencies will put their nose to the grindstone and really work for you.

8. DON'T DEMAND TOO MUCH

This can mean time from your agent, producer, development person, manager, or lawyer. It can also mean demanding too much money for yourself, and your particular project that may not warrant as big a deal as you want. Demanding a great deal of attention is another no-no. The Hollywood community is made up of a lot of very tough characters. They cannot get in and stay in without being very strong and determined. Demanding things that you haven't earned isn't a good way to get what you want. Once you earn it… you'll get it all.

9. DON'T DO DRUGS AND ALCOHOL

They will absolutely ruin your career. During my years as an agent I represented one drug addict and one alcoholic (as far as I know). They were both very talented people who destroyed their careers. By the time I found out about their addictions it was too late. At some point your problem will be discovered and you will never be let back in. When you are at a business social event keep your limit to two drinks or less. This way you will always be in control of what you say and do.

10. DON'T EVER THINK YOU ARE TOO BIG AND IMPORTANT TO WRITE MORE SPEC SCRIPTS

In the late 1990s I represented Dennis, a former actor who had become a writer. He had a modicum of success writing some low- and medium-budget independent feature films. I had introduced him to a director client of mine and they hit it off quite well. This director hired my writer on a couple of movies over a two-year period. I had repeatedly asked Dennis to come up with new ideas and spec screenplays. He refused to spec any scripts and the few pitch ideas he shared with me were not the least bit saleable. These ideas were far from what the studios were looking for. After many years of representing Dennis I received a call from him in November of 1997 wherein he demanded that I get him a writing gig before Christmas. He was speaking to me in an ill-tempered way, to say the least. I had always liked Dennis, and his wife, tremendously and had worked hard in the past to get jobs for him. His attitude, timing, and demands were shocking to me. I took a breath and replied that he hadn't given me a new piece of material in over five years and that there was no work for him now. Just before the Christmas holidays the film business slows down to a snail's pace. The production companies and studios are running low on their discretionary funds and everyone seems to want to spend their time planning and discussing their skiing trips and other vacation ideas. Sadly for me, and perhaps for him, we parted ways. Suffice it to say that Dennis's writing career has never taken off.

> **EXERCISES**

1. Stop rewriting that same project over and over.

2. Call to thank someone who has helped you.

3. Get your ideas in "pitching" shape by practicing with a friend.

4. Write brief treatments for all of your projects.

5. Ask someone you trust to read your work (no relatives) and then listen carefully to his or her advice.

SPECIAL TIPS FOR TELEVISION MOVIE WRITERS AND TELEVISION SERIES WRITERS

9

Most of this book may seem aimed solely at new writers of motion picture screenplays; however, the information I'm providing you can apply to all types of entertainment writers. It doesn't matter if you write television movies, television series, or feature films — you can still expect the same things from your agent, lawyer, and/or manager. These advisors still need to represent your best interests and negotiate on your behalf. Television series writers must have the same amount of "ammunition" to get into their field as movie writers. The relation ships, networking, socializing, writers' contracts, attitude, and hard work apply to all areas of the business.

That said, you'll need to adhere to some specific rules if you're going to aim your career in the television world successfully. Here is some important information that will help you.

TELEVISION MOVIES

1. To secure the services of an agent as well as to sell yourself as a TV movie writer, it is best to have a minimum of three sample scripts in the TV movie format and they should be your original ideas. In the event that your projects are based on true-life stories, then you must get the rights before you write the script (see point 4 below).

2. When writing sample television-movie scripts, try to keep the production costs fairly low. No multiple airplane crashes, no period pieces requiring extensive wardrobe appropriate to that period. It is also difficult to sell a TV movie that calls for multiple foreign locations. You will notice that most TV movies are set in the present, in unnamed cities, and deal primarily with emotional relationships.

3. When writing for television it is important that the main character of the piece must be on every page. This is the same as major motion pictures. The audience wants to follow that character and needs to care about his or her well-being.

4. If you decide that one of your samples must be a true story, you will have to secure the rights of the people involved, prior to attempting to sell the script. Producers don't want to be blindsided by someone who thinks that she can get hundreds of thousands of dollars for the rights to her life story. You must locate the rights holder(s) of the life story. This may be the story's subject, or his or her heirs. Next, you will have to negotiate a deal that is standard within the TV movie business. It is a long and complicated process that may also cost you money for an exclusive option and lawyer's fees, as well as a tremendous amount of your time. As in any negotiation, there are no guarantees that you will be able to secure the rights in a fair and equitable manner.

5. If you decide not to write an original teleplay, but opt instead to write an adaptation of a novel, you must have all of the rights to the novel secured prior to presenting the project to producers and/or networks and cable companies. There is a lot of work involved in getting these rights. You will need to research the original novel, find out who represents the rights, negotiate a deal that may require you to put up some "up-front" money out of your own pocket, hire lawyers to draw up a contract with the rights holder(s), and make sure that the contract is transferable in the event you are able to sell the project.

6. In the event that you are able to get some interest from agents and/or producers in this field, you will need to have meetings wherein you must be able to pitch more TV movie ideas. Make sure you have them ready and in treatment form so that you can leave them behind after the meetings.

7. Keep up with all TV movies. Watch old ones and new ones. Watch the made-for-TV movies on Lifetime, TNT, Sci-Fi, AMC, HBO, Showtime, and any other place you can find them. Get them from Blockbuster and/or Netflix or On-Demand. This is your job now. You must be knowledgeable about what productions companies produce and where they are aired. For example, you won't want to pitch a female-driven relationship project to TNT or HBO.

TV SERIES AND EPISODIC WRITING

1. When trying to break into the TV series business you will need at least three great writing samples. These need to be of shows that have been on the air for a minimum of two to three seasons. They should be for different series, but they must be shows that are in the same genre. Sample scripts should not be original pilots by you. Show runners are looking for new writers who can copy the "voices" of their show's characters and who know how to plot a show like theirs. If you are able to get a pitch meeting on a show you will be presenting different episode ideas that you hope the producers will hire you to write. If all goes well, they might give you one or two other chances to write episodes for the show. All of this is in the hope, both for them and for you, that you will be a good match and they will hire you to work on the show's staff.

2. To write and work for network television, you must live in the Los Angeles area, unless you are hired by a show that is shot elsewhere. Shows want writers who will join the staff and that means being nearby.

3. Writing a spec pilot prior to working on regular TV series is a waste of time and energy. The business isn't interested in show ideas from new writers. They want professional writers who have worked on staff and served as producers on shows. They need someone who can create a series and then run the show.

4. If you are able to get a pitch meeting with a show, be sure to be familiar with that particular series. It would be best if you came to the pitch meeting armed with about ten or twelve story ideas. Make

sure you are true to the characters. I was once lucky enough to get a pitch meeting for a new writer on the great series, *M★A★S★H*. She completely blew her meeting by bringing in her cat and by insisting that Hawkeye Pierce had a wife in the States. The producer couldn't get her, and her cat, out of there fast enough.

SAMPLE AGREEMENT: TV MOVIE SPEC SCRIPT

The following is a sampling of some of the main parts of an agreement for writing services and purchase of an original "spec" script for a television movie. This particular writer had formed a corporation we will refer to as "Riter, Inc." Also note that a tremendous amount of U.S. television movies are produced in Canada. The contract below is with a Canadian production company. It is a good sample of both U.S. and Canadian deals.

JONES PRODUCTIONS, INC.

Date:_____

Riter, Inc.

c/o The Best Agency

30000 Santa Monica Ave.

West Hollywood, CA 99998

RE: "THE COVE"/OPTION AND WRITING SERVICES
AGREEMENT

Dear Sirs:

This letter sets forth the terms of the agreement ("Agreement") between Jones Productions ("Producer") and Riter, Inc. ("Lender") furnishing the services of Jane Doe ("Artist"), regarding the grant of an option by Lender to Producer to acquire certain rights in and to that certain original unpublished script written by Artist entitled "The Cove" ("Script"), for use as the basis of a proposed movie-for-television currently also entitled "The Cove" (the "Movie"), and Producer's engagement of Lender to furnish additional writing services of Artist in connection with the Script, as follows:

1.   CONDITIONS PRECEDENT: Producer's obligations under this Agreement expressly subject to and conditioned upon the satisfaction of each of the following conditions precedent:

   1.1   Producer's receipt of an executed original of this Agreement;

   1.2   Producer's receipt of an executed original of a certificate of authorship substantially in Producer's standard form concerning Artist's writing services hereunder;

   1.3   Producer's receipt of an executed original of a Short Form Option Agreement in the form attached hereto as Exhibit "A"; and

   1.4   Producer's receipt of all applicable payroll and tax-related forms reasonably required by Producer.

A waiver by Producer of any of the foregoing conditions precedent will not be a waiver of any other condition precedent.

2. GRANT OF OPTION: Lender hereby grants to Producer the exclusive and irrevocable right and option ("Option"), for the "Option Period" and consideration specified in Paragraph 3, to purchase from Lender the "Granted rights" (as defined in Paragraph 6), upon the terms and conditions set forth in this Agreement.

3. OPTION PERIOD AND CONSIDERATION: As consideration for the Option and for all the representations, warranties and agreements made by Lender and Artist hereunder, Producer will pay to Lender the following amounts and the Option shall be effective during the following period ("Option Period"):

    3.1 Initial Option Period: Subject to extension as set forth below, the Option will be effective during the six (6) month period commencing August 7, 2002, and continuing through and including February 5, 2002 ("Initial Option Period"). Producer will pay Lender $XXX for the Initial Option Period, payable upon satisfaction of the conditions precedent set forth in Paragraph 1, which sum will not be applicable against the "Purchase Price" (as defined in Paragraph 7).

    3.2 Extended Option Period: Producer will have the right to extend the Initial Option Period for an additional period of six (6) months, through and including August 6, 2003 ("Extended Option Period"), by giving written notice thereof to Lender on or before the end of the Initial Option Period, accompanied by payment of the sum of US$XXX for the Extended Option Period, which sum will not be applicable against the Purchase Price.

    3.3 Development During Option Period: Lender and Artist agree that Producer will have the right throughout the

Option Period to engage in all customary development and preproduction activities in connection with the Script and the Movie (including without limitation engaging Lender to furnish Artist's writing services pursuant to Paragraph 4), for use in connection with the exploitation of any of the Granted Rights. All of the results and proceeds of any such activities will at all times be the sole and exclusive property of Producer whether or not the Option is exercised.

3.4 Claims/Force Majeure: If any event of force majeure occurs during the Option Period (e.g., any strike, lockout or other labour dispute, fire, war, governmental action or proceeding, injunction or any contingency beyond Producer's control) that affects any of the Granted Rights or Producer's development, financing, production or exploitation of motion pictures or programs, or any of Producer's normal business operations, or if Lender or Artist is in default or otherwise in breach of any representation, warranty or agreement made hereunder, or if any claim is asserted against Lender, Artist and/or Producer in connection with the Script, the Movie and/or any of the Granted Rights, then Producer will have the right, at Producer's election and without limiting Producer's other rights or remedies hereunder or at law or in equity, (1) to extend the Option Period and all other time periods hereunder for the duration of such event of force majeure, default or breach or claim; and/or (2) to terminate this Agreement and any or all of Producer's obligations hereunder (in which event Lender will return to Producer within five (5) days of such termination all Option payments theretofore paid to Lender by Producer).

4. WRITING SERVICES:

4.1 Rewrite: Subject to the satisfaction of each of the conditions precedent set forth in Paragraph 1, Producer hereby engages Lender to furnish the services of Artist to write a rewrite of the Script (the "Rewrite"), and Lender hereby accepts such engagement. As consideration for the Rewrite, Producer will pay Lender the sum of US$XXX, payable 50% promptly following commencement of the Rewrite and 50% promptly following delivery of the Rewrite, which sum will not be applicable against the "Purchase Price" (as defined in subparagraph 7.1(a).

4.2   Polish (Optional): Lender hereby grants to Producer the exclusive and irrevocable option to engage Lender to furnish the services of Artist to write a polish of the rewritten Script (the "Polish"). If Producer exercises such option, Producer will engage Lender to furnish the services of Artist to write the Polish, and Lender hereby agrees to accept such engagement. As consideration for the Polish, Producer will pay Lender the sum of US$XXX, promptly following delivery of the Polish, which payment will not be applicable against the Purchase Price.

4.3   Delivery: All writing will be delivered to Producer when reasonably required by Producer to enable Producer to review such writing and meet its production requirements. All official deliveries of any such writing hereunder must be made to the attention of Sally Smith at 8121 Charring Cross Road, Toronto, Canada. Any delivery of any materials written by Artist hereunder to a person or persons other than as set forth in the preceding sentence will not be deemed to satisfy delivery requirements for purposes of payment under this Agreement.

4.4   Other: Artist's services pursuant to this Paragraph 4 will commence on such date(s) as Producers designates in its sole discretion. Artist's services pursuant to this Paragraph 4 will be exclusive to Producer during any period when Artist is rendering services to Producer hereunder. Artist shall attend all rehearsals, conferences and other meetings at which Artist's presence is reasonably required by Producer.

4.5 <u>Work-for-Hire</u>: All of the results and proceeds of Artist's writing services hereunder, and all copyrights pertaining thereto and extensions and renewals thereof, are and will be the sole and exclusive property of Producer in perpetuity and in all languages throughout the universe and will constitute "work done in the course of employment" for Producer for purposes of Canadian copyright law and a "work-made-for-hire" for Producer specially ordered or commissioned by Producer for purposes of U.S. copyright law. To the extent such results and proceeds may ever be determined by a court of competent jurisdiction not to be a "work done in the course of employment" or "work-made-for-hire," as applicable, Lender and Artist hereby irrevocably and exclusively assign and/or grant to Producer, in consideration for the compensation provided hereunder, all right, title and interest thereto including without limitation all exclusive exploitation rights and copyright and associated rights herein and all extensions and renewals thereof throughout the universe in perpetuity.

5. <u>EXERCISE OF OPTION</u>: The Option may be exercised by written notice to Lender at any time during the Option Period. Whether or not Producer serves such notice, commencement of principal photography of the "Initial Production" (as defined in Paragraph 6) during the Option Period will be deemed to be the exercise of the Option and proper notice thereof. If Producer does not exercise the Option, then the Granted Rights will be retained by Lender and, at Lender's request, Producer will execute such documents as are reasonably necessary to evidence such effect.

6. <u>GRANTED RIGHTS</u>: Subject only to the exercise of the Option, Lender hereby irrevocably licenses exclusively to Producer, its successors, assigns and licensees, in perpetuity throughout

the universe, the right (the "Initial Production Rights") to produce a single production (the "Initial Production") based on
the Script, the Rewrite, the Polish (if any), and/or any further
written materials prepared by Artist in connection therewith,
if requested by Producer (collectively, the "Work"). In addition,
subject only to the exercise of the Option, Lender hereby irrevocably licenses exclusively to Producer, its successors, assigns
and licensees, in perpetuity throughout the universe all other
rights (the "Additional Rights") of every kind and nature in
and to the Work (the Initial Production Rights and the Additional Rights shall hereinafter collectively be referred to as
the "Granted Rights"). Without limiting the generality of the
foregoing licenses, the Granted Rights shall include the following: the right to develop, produce, distribute and otherwise exploit and turn to account one or more Motion Pictures
(including feature films, television movies, mini-series, episodic
series, sequels, prequels or remakes) based upon, adapted from
or inspired by the Work or any part thereof, in perpetuity
and throughout the universe, in any manner and all media,
whether now known or hereafter devised, as Producer in its sole
discretion shall determine, including, without limitation, theat-
rically, non-theatrically, on all forms of television (including,
without limitation, live, free, pay, cable, subscription, satellite,
advertisement, long form, series television rights and educa-
tional television) and on and by all forms of home video, DVD,
CD-ROM, CD-I and all analogous forms of media; the right
to develop, produce, present and exploit, in any manner and
all media, one or more Live Stage Productions based upon,
adapted from or inspired by the Work or any part thereof, in
perpetuity and throughout the universe; and the right to exploit and turn to account, in any manner, media and territory,
any and all radio rights, music publishing rights, novelization
rights, Interactive Multi-Media Electronic rights, On-Line Internet Rights, digital entertainment rights, animation rights,

video game rights, theme park rights, soundtrack recording rights, Commercial Tie-In Rights and Merchandising Rights, promotional and advertising rights and all other allied, ancillary, subsidiary and incidental rights of whatsoever kind or nature in and to the Work and the title thereof and/or any and all Motion Pictures and/or Live Stage Productions based hereon or adapted or inspired there from. In exercising the Granted Rights, Producer shall be entitled to translate the Work or any part thereof into any and all languages, to adapt, rearrange and make changes in, deletions from or additions to the Work, to change the sequence thereof, to use a portion or portions of the Work, to change the characters appearing therein and to change the descriptions of such characters and to use the title of the Work and the title or subtitle of any component of the Work as the title of any Motion Pictures and/or Live Stage Productions based thereon or adapted or inspired there from or as the title of any musical composition contained therein. To the maximum extent allowed, Lender and Artist hereby expressly waive in favor of Producer and its successors, assigns and licensees, in perpetuity, without limitation, any and all rights which Lender or Artist may have or claim to have with respect to the Work under any law relating to the "moral rights of authors" or any similar law throughout the universe or as a result of any alleged violation of said rights and Lender and Artist agree not to institute or authorize any action on the grounds that any changes, deletions, additions, or other use of the Work violate such rights or constitutes a defamation or mutilation of any part thereof. Notwithstanding the foregoing, Artists shall be consulted in respect of proposed changes and modifications to the Work pursuant to and in conformity with the requirements of Article B110 of the Writers Guild of Canada ("WGC") Independent Production Agreement entered into by the WGC and the Canadian Film and Television Production Association and the Association des Producteurs de Film et Television de Quebec, in force as of the date of this Agreement ("IPA"). Lender and Artist hereby consent to any change of the title of the Initial Production that Producer may decide to make. Producer may take all necessary steps to register in any and all jurisdictions the rights granted to Producer hereunder and to register the copyright in and to any Motion Pictures and/or Live Stage Productions based upon, adapted from or inspired by the Work. Other than as expressly set out herein, there shall be no reversion of any rights or licenses granted under this Agreement without the express prior written consent of Producer.

7.   <u>CONSIDERATION</u>: As consideration in full for the Granted Rights and for the representations, warranties and agreements made by Lender and Artist hereunder, if Producer exercises the Option, Producer will pay Lender the following amounts:

7.1   In respect of the Initial Production Rights:

    i. within ten (10) business days after exercise of the Option, the sum of US$XX (the "Purchase Price");

    ii. a "Production Fee" (as defined in the IPA) in connection with the Initial Production, if any, calculated in accordance with Article C10 of the IPA, which amount may be offset by Producer against the Purchase Price in accordance with Section C1007 of the IPA, if applicable; and

    iii. except as may be otherwise provided in the "Waiver" (as defined in Paragraph 8.3 hereof), a "Distribution Royalty" (as defined in the IPA), if any, in connection with the Initial Production, if any, calculated in accordance with Article C11 of the IPA (provided that, to the maximum extent permitted under the IPA, all amounts paid to Lender hereunder shall be applied against such Distribution Royalty).

7.2   In respect of the Additional rights:

(a) Within ten (10) days after the exercise of the Option, the additional sum of ten U.S. dollars (US$10.00).

7.3.   To the extent Lender is entitled to receive any payments pursuant to Article B113(a) of the IPA, such payments shall be paid at the rate of 15% of the minimum "Script Fee" as set forth in Article C301 of the IPA ("Minimum Script Fee"), and to the extent Lender is entitled to receive any payments pursuant to Article B113(b), of the IPA, such payment shall be paid at the rate of 7.5% of the Minimum Script Fee for each character, to a maximum of 15% (as set forth in Article B113(c)(i) and (ii).

7.4.   If Producer wishes to use the Work as the basis of a series, Producer may acquire the license provided for in Article B114 of the IPA by payment to Lender of 50% of the Minimum Script Fee.

7.5.   Without limiting or restricting any other terms set forth herein, in consideration of the sum of two U.S. dollars (US$2.00) and other good and valuable consideration, the receipt and sufficiency of which are hereby acknowledged, Lender hereby agrees that Producer shall be entitled to commission or engage any subsequent writer to perform any of the services set forth in Article B108 of the IPA, without any additional payments to Lender or Artist.

8.   GUILD AGREEMENT:

8.1.   This Agreement will be governed by the terms and conditions of the IPA.

8.2.   Producer is entitled to the maximum rights under the IPA and it is obligated to make the minimum payments and Producer shall have the right to make and/or apply over-scale compensating against other minimum compensation due Lender under this Agreement to the maximum extent permitted pursuant to the IPA.

8.3. Pursuant to the reciprocal agreement between the WGC and the Writers Guild of America (the "WGA"), this engagement will be further subject to the jurisdiction of the WGA with a Working Rule 8 Waiver ("Waiver"). Lender agrees to cooperate and execute all required documents to facilitate the Waiver and to use Lender's best efforts to obtain the Waiver. Provided that Lender provides Producer with the Waiver:

(a) Producer will make all required pension, health and welfare payments to the WGA for the writing fees for the Movie, in which case, Producer will have no obligation to make any contributions to the WGC in respect thereto as would otherwise be required under Article A13 of the IPA on behalf of Lender or Artist;

(b The Purchase Price will be applied against any sums required to be paid to Lender pursuant to the Waiver, including without limitation, against any amounts paid to it by way of any WGA residuals, separation of rights payments, royalties, character royalties and other like payments due to Lender pursuant to the Waiver. If Producer produces the Initial Production for initial exhibition on a basic cable channel, and provided Artists receives writing credit thereon, Producer will pay residuals pursuant to the WGA Basic Agreement, which will be calculated in accordance with the so-called "Sanchez Formula" (as described in subparagraph 2.b.[1] of Appendix C to the WGA Basic Agreement.

9. CREDIT: On condition that neither Lender nor Artist is in default or otherwise in material breach hereof, and subject to network and guild approvals and restrictions, Producer will accord Artist credit pursuant to the IPA. Subject to the foregoing, the size, style, type, placement and all other matters pertaining

to credits will be determined by Producer in its sole discretion. No casual, inadvertent or unintentional failure by Producer to comply with the credit provisions hereof, nor any failure by any third party to comply with such credit provisions, will constitute a breach by Producer of this Agreement.

• • •

There are other points and conditions to this contract; however, I believe that the above will give you the gist of the agreements made between you, as a writer, and a producer and/or production company.

WINNING THE NETWORKING GAME 10

There's that awful term again: *networking*. It's thrown around in every seminar you attend, in every how-to book you read, and by every writer you know. They all say it's the way to get in, the way to keep up, to get ahead and to keep current. You're told it's something you must do or you won't have a writing career. All of these things are true. Unfortunately, up until now, no one has explained exactly how to do it.

Networking is nothing more than pushing yourself a little harder to socialize within a business that you love. It's not as difficult or stressful as it seems and can often be fun and extremely rewarding. It's about making new friends (aka *contacts*) who will add to your life as well as your career.

I've spent most of my business life guiding the careers of writers, directors, and producers. As an agent I've submitted scripts, negotiated deals, advised clients, worked with projects, edited properties, and sold hundreds and hundreds of hours of motion pictures, movies for television, miniseries, and television series. I've also been the one to fan the flames for clients to make sure that they stayed hot. To keep those fires burning it takes both the agent and the client. To do all of these things I had to get over being a shy person. I had to train myself to reach out to strangers and make those cold calls. Most people think of themselves as shy or a bit reserved. Sometimes the people who appear to be the most outgoing were often the most introverted kids in class.

If I could do it so can you.

You're probably a solo worker by virtue of being a writer. Perhaps you've always been shy or afraid you'll say the wrong thing.

Another problem you may have in networking is that you live in Minnesota or Alaska, or Anytown, USA, where you think you can't get to all those industry professionals, who live in Hollywood and Beverly Hills.

Networking is a learned and practiced skill. If you follow the points below, you will be able to network with anyone, anywhere.

a. Remember that you have something to offer and the people you meet might actually want to talk to you.

b. Know that you have nothing to lose. The worst thing that can happen is that the people you try to meet will be rude. You can live with a little rudeness, can't you?

c. Be aware that you might add something to someone else's life and that you might find some common ground.

d. Acknowledge to yourself that the other person may also be shy.

e. Everyone likes to talk about him- or herself. Ask lots of questions like: "How long have you been in the business?" or "How did you get started?" or "Do you like your work?" These questions work like a charm.

POTENTIAL CONTACTS ARE EVERYWHERE

I understand that you may not be sure where and who these magical people are with whom you must network. To really network in the most productive way is to find those people who seem impossible to find. You know they are out there, but how do you get to them? Why will they want to talk to you?

It's one thing to give your projects to friends or family to critique. You may even join a writers' group or post your work on the ubiquitous Internet. Perhaps you have used a professional consultant to help with your work. Is this networking? The simple answer is yes and no.

Hollywood is in the business of finding the best clients, screenplays, novels, writers, and talent of all sorts. They certainly work hard to reach out to new writers with lots of talent and great ideas. These people search near and far to find the project they can sell or the brilliant writer they can represent. Don't believe that they are not open to you, because they are.

Finding them isn't all that difficult. They are everywhere. They're listed with the Writers Guild of America; they're on the Internet and in numerous published information guides like *The Hollywood Creative Directory*. These industry insiders speak at seminars and on panels; they go to every film festival in the world. They are right in front of you.

Armed with this information, the next and most important steps are up to you.

THE SIX BASIC QUESTIONS OF NETWORKING
Who?

Since the best connections are out there in your universe you must attend every bona fide seminar, film festival, writers' conference, panel discussion, and speaker series that you possibly can find. Everyone at these events is a potential *contact*. The guest speakers or panel members who come to these events to hear your pitches are usually agents, producers, development executives, script consultants, professional writers, directors, and film financiers. These people are solid gold to you. Every speaker has come to help you with your career and in exchange is looking for a great project and/or client.

Always have a business card to trade with each speaker and everyone else you meet. Yours may simply state your name, address, phone number, and email address, and the word "Writer." Don't worry; you don't have to be a sold writer to make a business card. Whether you sell or not, you do write. When you meet a potential contact, it is imperative that you ask for his or her business card; if he or she doesn't have one, ask for an email address and write it on a piece of paper for yourself.

Try to engage these people in a brief conversation. Compliment their speech or their work, and tell them a little bit about yourself. If you don't open up at all, you will easily be forgotten. Tell a funny story about your writing, or about your childhood, or how you met your significant other. Tell them anything that they might remember or that you can remind them about at a later date. Ask them a question or two about their work or where they are from. Do not hog their time. If their eyes start to wander, thank them for their time and walk away.

If you are lucky enough to live in the Los Angeles area you are sure to know someone who knows someone who knows someone in the movie business. Try to connect to that person to see if he or she can help you. Let it be known that you are a screenwriter and that you want your material read. You will be amazed to discover that if you let people know what you want, they will try to help you. You'll probably find an important agent sitting next to you at your local Starbuck's... start a conversation... take a chance.

What?

The contacts you make are your doorways into the mainstream of your writing career. To follow up with those contacts you need to email or phone them regarding your best project. By doing this you are taking your second most important step to your success. (Naturally, having your finished project is the first step.)

Whenever you pitch a screenplay at a writers' conference, it must be a project that you have already completed and is ready to be shown. If the person you are pitching to likes the idea and wants to see it, you must send it to him or her immediately. Timing is everything. What is hot now will not be hot in a month. The agent or producer will have forgotten you and the idea if you wait too long and your script will end up in the dead pile of unread scripts. You only get one chance with these people — use it wisely.

When?

Every chance you get to interface with industry professionals is the right time to act. Whether your project is finished or not, it is in your best interest to make the person-to-person contact and hold on to his or her information (i.e., business card) until you are ready to submit something wonderful to him or her. Try to make a positive personal impression even if you don't wind up pitching. Entering some film contests is also a great way to connect. You will have your material read by excellent people who will jump at the chance to get to you if your script is outstanding.

If you see the same people at more than one event, you should remind them that you've met before.

Where?

You need to go anywhere you can to find professionals as well as other writers. Don't ignore new writers' groups, Internet groups, even magazines and books that list all those many, many conferences and festivals. Going to these events will be money well spent on your career. Wherever you live, there are sure to be some conferences in your home state or not too far from your hometown. Try local universities to see if any of their classes have guest speakers from Hollywood.

Why?

If you don't connect and network, your work will sit on your shelf or in your closet and only be read by your family and friends. If you really want your work published or seen on the screen, you must make contact with these people. There is no magic way to circumvent this route. To be sold, your work must be seen by the right people. Only you can make this happen.

How?

After trading those wonderful little business cards that I mentioned in the "Who?" section of this chapter, you need to send a short thank you note to reintroduce yourself to those speakers, panelists, etc. It is the best way to stay in touch with those people and a lovely way to let them know that their work was recognized and appreciated. Remember that everyone likes, wants, and needs to be valued for their efforts. If you have a script that is ready, ask if you may send it to them. Put a one- or two-paragraph synopsis in your thank-you note. If you get to pitch your script at a conference and if their response is positive be sure to submit your project in a timely manner. That means the very next day. When you send the script, you need to remind them in your cover letter that they said you could send the script to them. Whether they look at your script or not, the next step is to ask for a meeting to discuss your work, and to pitch new ideas to them. It is paramount to keep up some sort of sporadic communication with these people, even if it's a birthday or Christmas card. You have to let them know that you are not just going to fade away. One of them will be able to move your work forward, get it to someone who can say "yes," or even just give you great advice… we all need someone in our corner.

Following up with people is essential. Most industry professionals will not call you even if they said they would when you met. You must make those follow-up calls and emails yourself. Once you've sent your material, wait about two weeks to email them and ask if they've received it and if anyone has had a chance to look at it yet. If the answer is no, then wait another two weeks and email again.

REAPING THE BENEFITS OF NETWORKING

Networking is simply a business activity that is paramount to your success. People who may be important for you are everywhere and you may find new friends who are willing and able to help you in many ways. If you are sitting in a seminar you may be seated next to a new writer who happens to know a great script consultant and who has great connections in the Hollywood community. Even other new writers may end up being good connections. Exchange cards with everyone you meet at these events and start emailing each other and sharing news and information. With the world growing smaller and smaller by virtue of email and Internet information you have great access at your fingertips.

When I was an agent I had to make "cold calls" almost every day of my life. Cold calling is just another term for networking. It was one of the most difficult parts of my job, but I did it anyway. I had to do it for my clients. To put it simply, because something is difficult or makes you nervous is no reason not to do it. We are in a tough business and you must learn to toughen up.

Once you have mastered the art of networking it will be a skill that will work for you forever. It will continue to help you personally as well as in your professional life. When you network, you connect, enriching your own life as well as your contact's.

I often used my networking skills in a casual setting to help my clients get jobs. In 1987, while representing Larry Hertzog, who was, at that time, a producer for Stephen J. Cannell Productions on a show titled *J. J. Starbuck*, I had just signed a new writer by the name of Randall Wallace (yes, he's the one who went on to write *Braveheart*, *Pearl Harbor*, *The Man in the Iron Mask*, etc.). He was the kind of "good ole boy" I knew would be a perfect staff writer for *J. J. Starbuck*. Since Randy had no writing credentials at that time, it would have been very difficult to get him a writing assignment. I decided to invite both Larry and Randy to my home for dinner. By the end of the evening Randy had a job. Larry only stipulated that he needed to read a writing sample. I was sure that Larry would be quite impressed with Randy's spec script, and he was. It was the start of a very long and prolific career for Randy Wallace.

Many writers obtained work over my dining room table. It was networking at its best because people had fun, and felt relaxed. No one sitting in the "power" chair behind a desk. There was a feeling of equality.

Networking can happen in many circumstances. If you are attending a seminar make sure to introduce yourself to whomever is sitting next to you, on both sides; exchange cards and follow up with emails just saying hello. You never know where the next bit of great information will come from.

This business is all about taking chances. From the first writing class to making your latest deal, it's all a gamble. Go ahead, toss those dice.

> **EXERCISES**

1. Get business cards made.

2. Sign up to hear a seminar on writing or attend a conference.

3. Approach the speakers at the conference or seminar, exchange cards, and send a follow-up thank-you letter.

4. Practice introducing yourself and pitching your movie idea.

SOCIALIZING

11

Socializing is an extension of networking, but is not the same thing. It goes beyond, to the next step, in helping to ensure that you maintain a long life in professional writing. Working in Hollywood is not only about the quality of your work, but it is about living in the entertainment community. You will want to forge friendships and social connections with others who also live in the world of movies and television.

Networking provides the initial entrée through these proverbially closed doors of show business. Socializing allows you to establish relationships with the Tinseltown folks who are necessary to your future after you've come through those doors. Your shared love for the business will naturally draw you together.

You might think that writing well and even having a hit movie is enough. Not a chance, folks. One-hit-wonders are a dime a dozen in every business. If you want to have staying power you'll need friends who will give you the benefit of their knowledge and connections. Industry insiders spend an inordinate amount of time at activities that look like simple socializing interactions. The truth is that they are always working. Executives have breakfast, lunch, drinks, and dinner meetings. They attend dinner parties, galas, award ceremonies, cocktail parties, and screenings. Personally, I often found these events both physically and emotionally draining because while they looked glamorous and fun, they were really hard work. For example, the person you are talking to may be looking over your shoulder to see whom else she wants to speak with. The person you want to talk with may be too difficult to get close to or too busy with others. The hours are late and it's usually been a long day. The wannabes are all over the place and vying for your attention.

The good that can come from these events might be that an agent may run into someone who is interested in his or her client's projects. A writer might meet some industry executive he or she really likes and who may want to work with that writer extensively in the future. There are endless positive things that can and often do happen at these social events. So, we go and go and go to as many as possible. This means you have to go to these occasions too.

For writers, socializing is a combination of hanging out and going out. If you meet someone in the business you are fortunate enough to like, you might have to make the first move and see if he or she wants to join you for coffee or perhaps for lunch. If you have the ability to throw dinner or cocktail parties, then you must do that. I've found that mixing people who are in and out of the business is not a very good idea. Show people tend to want to talk to others in the same or similar fields of endeavor. Show business people talk in show business. That's our language, that's where we are comfortable and that's the subject in which we are most interested.

Earlier in this book I mentioned that I often orchestrated dinner parties and lunches so that my clients could meet buyers. Not every agent does this, but it's a good idea to ask your agent to try to put you together socially with development executives and producers. These are the people you will need. Remember the old saying, "The squeaky wheel gets the oil." All you can do is ask and if your agent doesn't do it then it's up to you to make it happen.

Whenever you are able to attend some social event you must never drink too much, talk too much, or do any drugs at all. The aforementioned also applies to your spouse or date who is attending with you. This kind of bad behavior will be remembered and you will never be trusted — certainly not with a writing assignment.

When you are fortunate enough to attend events you will need to mention your projects. Don't be shy about it. Everyone will want to hear a little bit about them and then they will want to put in their two cents on the creative aspects or saleability of those projects. Occasionally these folks will discuss their tennis or golf game, or their personal lives, but not much. We all want to talk about our projects and to hear about others. Ask them questions about their work, the companies they work for, and their favorite films and they will become your best friends.

I don't mean to tell you to befriend people you don't like. You will find there are plenty of those lurking about and you don't need to pursue them. Find people you enjoy and simply pursue a friendship. Remember that in business — just like in childhood — it's always good to use the buddy system.

I've met some of my best business friends at these kinds of events and it made my working life easier and much more pleasant. I ask about their children and spouses, their parents, and their favorite books. These are effortless ways to begin what could be very fortuitous associations.

Always keep in mind that you might be able to help someone else while you are looking for people to help you. As a writer you might have meetings where you find out information about job openings for development executives or what new projects are being developed. These are not secrets and if you share the information the recipients will "owe you one."

All of the above presupposes that you live in Los Angeles or its environs. Obviously, if you are living somewhere that's far from the action it will be nearly impossible for you to socialize in a meaningful way. Don't forget that people important to your future work often travel to your towns to give seminars and speeches and you could certainly invite them out for coffee. Then there's always Facebook and Twitter.

It is possible to have a script optioned if you live anywhere but the continuation of your writing career means that you must be able to reach out and touch the right people. A writing career is not defined by selling (optioning) screenplays. A writing career means meetings, writing assignments, and pitching to studio executives and to producers and development execs, in person. It means building a foundation with your agent and others in your working world. It means getting rewrite jobs and development assignments. These are the things that will keep you in front of the pack.

For writers, socializing can be more difficult than writing. I understand that these pointers are hard for you to think about and even harder to act upon. You'll simply have to focus on getting over your shyness.

So, get off your duffs and call someone.

> EXERCISES

1. Reach out to your writing group and invite some of them to dinner.

2. Go to a seminar and invite one or two of the speakers to lunch or coffee.

3. Take your script consultant to lunch.

GET YOUR QUERY LETTER READ, OR BUST

12

Everyone talks about the importance of the *query letter*. It is important because it may be the first introduction of you and your work to professionals in the entertainment business. We all know that first impressions are the ones that last. The query letter can make or break your chance at getting read. There are so many things you need to accomplish with this one page:

a. You want to motivate people who are extremely busy to spend their time, or the time of their employees, to read your screenplay.

b. You want them to know that you are serious about your work.

c. You want them to know that you have done a great job with your writing work.

d. You want them to think that if they don't read your script, they will miss a great opportunity.

It's a smart idea to let the recipient know that you haven't simply sent your query letter to a list of agents or producers (even if you have). Try to find information on the individual recipients so that you address them by name, not "Dear Sir" or "Dear Madam." Send letters to people you've heard speak at seminars, film festivals, and conferences. This way you will single them out. You may also find out who some of the agents represent, or some of the movies that the producers have produced, so you can mention how much you admire those films. You might simply mention that you've heard about their fine reputation.

Writers often feel stumped by the style, significance, and length of this particular missive. Take the following information to heart: If your letter is sloppy, you're out; if there are misspellings, you're out; if your grammar is poor, you're out; if your story idea is unclear or too long, you're out; if you tell too much about yourself, you're out.

As an agent I received thousands of query letters over the years. They arrived every day. The worst letter I have ever received began: "I have wrote a script." Now what do you think I did with that letter? That's right, the circular file. It hit the trash before I reached the writer's name. You might think that this sort of letter from a writer is impossible, but it was real, and it wasn't the only poorly written cover letter that I have received.

Sometimes the writers go on and on about themselves or their work. Sometimes they tell nothing about themselves or their work. Either way is bad. People only want to know things that are connected with your writing.

Here's the story of a good query letter:

Many years ago I was feeling very low because the latest writers' strike had almost ruined my business. One morning, while going through my mail, I read a simple query letter. It was perfect. The writer told me a little bit about himself. He had attended film school at USC and was from a tiny town in Alaska. He then added two paragraphs that told about his latest screenplay. It was a fascinating, contemporary, action-thriller, about the discovery of the Garden of Eden. There were no misspellings, no grammatical errors, no cross-outs, and no superfluous information. I grabbed the phone, called him, and asked him to send in the script.

I read the script the day that it arrived. It was wonderful, creative, smart, interesting, very well-formatted and professional. It also had heart and amazing visual potential. I phoned him before I even finished the script and made an appointment for him come in to meet with me the very next day. At that point in his life he and his wife were so broke that they were selling their CDs to buy gas for their beat-up old truck.

We met and discussed his many, many other ideas and completed screenplays. We signed contracts and I went to work calling production companies about this fabulous new client of mine and his amazing new original screenplay. Everyone I called wanted to see it immediately.

Within a couple of days my phone was ringing off the hook from other production companies and studio executives who had heard about this script and wanted to read it. I was thrilled.

Disney Studios stepped up to the plate and I made a deal for this young writer's first sale, for $750,000, plus profits. It was the beginning of a great career.

Your query letter is your introduction. It tells the reader who you are and what you have to offer. Paying attention to what seems to be a small thing in life can sometimes mean everything. Keep it direct, simple, and to the point. Be confident but not obnoxiously aggressive.

Remember that most query letters do not receive a reply. This is simply standard operating procedure and not personal. The recipients are too busy, their client list is full, they may not be taking new writers, they may not respond well to sci-fi or comedies or whatever you may have pitched, they may have the flu, they may be in a bad mood or are about to be fired. The reasons are too numerous to mention. You must follow up by calling the people to whom you've sent your query. Following up is the key to success in every field.

The query letter is only one of many ways of getting your script read, other than by your relatives. There are so many ways to get the attention of agent and producers. Some are a little too out there. For example, one day, when I worked at International Famous Agency (now known as ICM), I stepped off of the elevator into our reception area on the eighth floor of our offices on Sunset Boulevard, and there was a group of people dressed in space suits singing rock 'n' roll. They were trying to get representation from our music department, who casually ignored them. This was only one of many rather odd occurrences that took place. Personally I thought it was great fun.

Over the years I have received query letters filled with toys, flowers, jewelry, promises, pleading, and begging. I have not been moved by any of these.

Here is a sample query letter that says it all and has a little "personality" to boot:

SALLY SMITH
2100 Wilshire Boulevard
Los Angeles, CA 99999

March 1, 2010
John/Jane Doe
10000 Wilshire Boulevard
Los Angeles, CA 99999

Re: "NAME OF SCREENPLAY" written by Sally Smith

Dear Ms./Mr. Doe:

Hearing you speak at the _____ Writers Conference (Film Festival, etc.), I was very inspired by your remarks and your willingness to share information.

My background as a writer consists of studying screenwriting at UCLA, winning the _____ _____ screenwriting contest and practicing the craft of writing since I was ten years old. My spelling has improved, as well as my stories.

My original screenplay is a terrific, contemporary action/romance that tells the story of a young man and young woman who meet and fall in love during a cataclysmic event that sets them on a course to preserve the United States as an independent country.

I will call you next week to see if you are interested in reading my script.

Regards,

Sally Smith
Phone: _____Email: _____

> EXERCISES

1. Write three different query letters.

2. Edit them down to no more than one page in length.

3. Describe your screenplay story in one paragraph.

4. Double-check grammar and spelling.

5. Try to grab the reader in the first sentence.

THE INS AND OUTS OF PACKAGING

13

In the hopes of selling a screenplay many writers turn to packaging to enhance their projects. They are told that bringing in an actor or director will make producers want to buy their material. What few people understand is that the only way to really package a film is to bring in what is known as "A-list" talent. That means that if you attach a non-star actor or director you will be hurting a possible sale rather than helping it.

What makes it so difficult to package a project is that most people don't have direct access to the biggest stars. These people will only look at projects if there is an offer attached. Stars also want a major studio or financier and a great director.

Star actors will literally count their lines in a script. If there are not enough, they will pass on the project. They must also be in every scene. These are the rules. Without writing with these things in mind you will never get a major star for your movie.

The really tricky part of attaching actors or directors is to know who is really hot at any given moment. Except for true industry insiders, no one is privy to what is going on behind the scenes in the chaotic lives of stars. You might think that Star X would be great for the lead in your movie; however, what you probably won't know is that he may have a drug or alcohol problem, or that the studios can't get insurance on him because of some prior acts that have been kept quiet. You also won't know who has fallen out of favor, or gone cold at the box office, in the minds of the studio heads.

The big agencies are famous for their packaging departments and expertise. This work is only done if they represent the writer, star, and director. If you are signed with CAA and you think that a William Morris Endeavor star client would be perfect for your project, then you will probably be sorely disappointed. The point of packaging is not only to get a project produced, but for the agency to make a ton of money by using their own clients. Once again we are reminded that this is show *business*, not show *fun*.

A very important bit of information is that only the biggest and most successful elements (writers, stars, producers, directors) are used in a package. If you are not on the A-list, you will not be placed in the project. When trying to win over new clients, agencies that package may imply that they will slot you into their packages. Sorry to be the one to tell you, but this won't happen.

The best place to go for packaging your projects is to the great producers in Hollywood — the ones with excellent track records for producing big, hit films with big name stars. You need to get to them and trust that they will be able to put all of the right elements together to get the picture financed and produced. It is, after all, what they live for. This is where your agent comes into play in the best way. They know these producers and can get your projects read by them.

It is possible to package a low-budget film with some B-list actors. These are the recognizable actors who often play character roles in big movies. These wonderful people will often take a chance on a good script with a challenging role for them. Independent financiers will be more inclined to put up money for a film with known actors attached, even if those actors are on the B-list.

Producers look for good scripts from big agencies and small ones. They know that the next great writer may have been found by any agency. The smart ones keep their doors open to everyone, and most producers are very smart people.

II GETTING IN

IS THAT AN AGENT BEHIND YOU?

14

So here you are with a great script under your arm and not one Hollywood insider to read it. You just know a big Hollywood agent will want to sign you and soon you will have your first million-dollar sale. You can picture your name in big headlines in *Variety* and *The Hollywood Reporter*, proclaiming your gigantic sale. But wait, you're not so sure of the next step to take toward fulfilling those goals and dreams. There seem to be so many options and your friends, teachers and those fascinating script magazines offer such disparate advice. "Good grief," you say to yourself, "where do I go to find an agent? How do I know if they are a good agency? Will they even consider me? Do I just mail it or email them or send a query letter or call them? Will any of these things work?" The entire process seems so overwhelming.

"Perhaps," you think, "I should try to find someone to finance my movie project or, possibly, I could enter my screenplay at the Cannes Film Festival." You might consider sending those good query letters to hundreds of agents, but how, you wonder, do you know who and where they are? You might even start to think that you don't need some big hotshot Hollywood agent. Maybe you'll meet someone who knows someone who wants to direct a movie in your hometown. After all, you live in Minnesota or Scottsdale or Italy or Belgium. The elusive world of Hollywood is so terribly far away.

Stay with me here, it's not an impossible dream. People do it all the time.

First of all you need to live in or move to Los Angeles or New York. Preferably you should be in Los Angeles or within one hour's driving time from the city. Los Angeles is the home of the creative forces of the television networks, cable companies, motion picture studios, production companies, and independent producers. This is where the agents and managers live and work, eat and sleep, and socialize. This is where the magic happens. I know that moving to another city is a tremendous step to take, but it is a necessary one.

People will tell you about famous and successful writers who live in their hometowns. Believe me, there are extenuating circumstances. Perhaps some of those people made their mark while living in Hollywood and then moved back home, or they sold a novel and were hired to write the screenplay version. These are only a few of the scenarios that may have happened. In general it is best not to listen to others. People will tell you all sorts of bogus information. If you don't live in the greater Los Angeles area, you won't have a writing career. If you aren't conveniently located for last minute meetings, you will be too easily forgotten and replaced with the writers who are here.

Don't tell me that you will move here after you sell your first script. The system doesn't work that way very often. The only way most agents will even consider looking at a script that is written by an out-of-towner would be if it has been previously read by someone he or she knows and respects in the entertainment business *and* if the writer is incredibly prolific (which means you have already written five other screenplays and are in the middle of another one.) Okay, I know that most of you are going to ignore me on this so let's just move along.

Wherever you live, you need to know whether you are ready for and worthy of an agent. Aha! Never thought of that, did you? Well, they are not handed out like hors d'œuvres at a buffet. Not everyone gets one and not everyone is entitled to one. You have to earn your agent. Nose to the grindstone, fingers at the computer, rewrite 'til you can't see straight. Complete one spec script after another until you finally start to become a really, really good writer. Then and only then, you might get someone's assistant to take a look at your work. Be grateful if this happens because this may be your only way through those magic doors to success.

If you are wondering if you can survive in Hollywood without an agent, the answer is no, not really. Agents, and sometimes managers, are the only links to the real business of making movies and television. Agents are the keys to your success and survival. Not only do they know everyone, they also are your teachers, mentors, advisors, readers, consultants, connections, and negotiators. Without them you will be alone in wonderland or dealing with the fringe elements that will eat you up alive.

The fringe people are those who want to get into the mainstream of motion pictures and television, but haven't been able to make that leap. They will try to get you to write for free. They will tell you that they have great connections, when they don't. They will try to raise money with your material without protecting you in any way. Without an agent it is often difficult to discern who the interlopers are and who the bona fide producers are. Check people out in the *Hollywood Creative Directory* or simply call the Writers Guild of America for information.

It is tough to get to the top in any field of business. It's impossible, in the entertainment business, without an agent.

The personal problems of being a writer are huge. Your family will never understand why you don't simply get a job like everyone else. Your husband or wife will constantly interrupt you to run errands because you are writing at home (not really working). They might actually be a little ashamed of you because you are over thirty and not making a good living. You might be torn between getting a "real" job and continuing to try to make it as a professional writer.

The emotional side can be the most devastating of all. You give yourself time limits and have such high expectations. You get those dreadful rejection letters or, worse yet, no replies at all. You work like a dog for no foreseeable reward. You wonder why you are doing it, you get depressed, your girlfriend or boyfriend or even spouse walks out (I heard that Alex Haley's wife left him before he finished *Roots*).

Then… one day… your phone rings. The agent you wanted would like to sign you, or it's Warner Bros. with a huge offer, or a gigantic star wants to be in your picture, or Paramount wants to offer you a three-picture deal. They love you. You're a hit. Yes, it happens all the time. I've seen it happen and I've helped make it happen. It's glorious for everyone involved.

Years ago I was the first agent for a young writer named Carol Mendelsohn. She had a good spec script and I liked her. My client, Mike McGreevey, the producer of the TV series, *Fame*, had given her an assignment. He liked her work but didn't have any more assignments to give out at that moment. I invited Carol out to lunch along with my client, Larry Hertzog, who was then producing *Hardcastle and McCormick*, a series at Cannell Productions. Just as I knew they would, they hit it off right away. Carol went to work for Larry and of course is now famous for having co-created all of the *CSI* shows. She went from nowhere to a millionaire right in front of my eyes.

No matter what you hear, please believe that good literary agents are always looking for good writers. They are hard to find. Just as you want agents, they want and desperately need you. There is a quid pro quo to the agent-client relationship. If you are a success, then they are a success. We need each other.

It is an unfortunate law of the business that clients change agents, or go dry with their writing, or fall out of favor with the people in buying positions, or make the wrong enemies in L.A. This brings a void to the agent's client list. You can fill that void.

It's a great feeling to discover a new talent. I've been blessed with having that happen many, many times during my years as an agent.

As you can see, you must have an agent to really succeed in your writing career. To attract the agent who will best serve your interests, you need to bring exciting, unique, well-presented work to the table.

> **EXERCISES**

1. Go over your manuscripts and find the best two.

2. Rewrite those two pieces to prepare to submit them to agents.

3. If possible, use a good writer's consultant to find out if your screenplays are ready to be seen by professionals.

4. Get a copy of the *Hollywood Creative Directory/Representation* edition and review the various agencies.

WHAT DOES AN AGENT DO ALL DAY? 15

Okay, so now you know that you need an agent, but you may not know exactly what an agent does for you.

THE THREE S'S OF AGENTING

Individual agents are responsible to their agencies for what are known as the three "S's" of representation. They are:

1. Signing
2. Servicing
3. Selling

That's it. It sounds simple, but it isn't. The amount of responsibility an agent carries is largely dependent upon the agency's size and scope.

Defining the three "S's" of agenting is easy. As you will see, carrying them out can be complicated.

Signing

Agents must constantly research all of the best working writers in town – writers who have the potential to bring money into the agency. Agents need to find out who represents these writers, if they are happy with their current representation, or if they are getting a little itchy to move on to someone else. Getting this kind of information takes lots of contacts and personal relationships.

Then the agent must launch an attack to lure the client. That means getting to the writer, taking him or her out to lunches, dinners, drinks, Hollywood parties, screenings and more. It requires a modicum of charm and deceit. The deceit is in "stealing" a writer from another agency that may be representing the client efficiently. The new agent needs to assure the writer that he or she will do a much better job for the client than anyone else. The "charm" part of this formula lies in being able to coax a seemingly content writer to choose a new agency over his or her old one.

Signing also requires knowing who all of the hot "newbie" writers are and trying to get them. That means going to screenings of independent films, film festivals, and new writer seminars. It means reading all of the new material that is getting some heat.

Signing also means being a "closer." An agent may be able to woo a great writer, but may often be unable to tear them away from the agent that currently represents them. There is a great deal of pressure from the heads of their departments to close in on these writers by getting them to sign on the dotted line.

As you can imagine, all of the above takes a great deal of time.

Servicing

This entails keeping your current clients happy. Wining and dining them is important as well as winning your client's confidence and trust. Agents must read all of a client's new material. In some of the large agencies they will also have to read a synopsis of the new material brought in by the clients of other agents in their department. Agents must spend time going over new story ideas, treatments, spec scripts, and pitches with all of their clients. Servicing may often mean listening to a client's personal problems, philosophies, and interests. It may include going to clients' weddings, their kids' bar mitzvahs, confirmations, and many other personal and family occasions. It means making sure your assistant knows the birthdays of your biggest moneymakers. It means having flowers sent if a client has her appendix removed. Agents only get this involved with clients if they are very big earners for the agency. The expense accounts are reviewed and often questioned. If the client receiving flowers or lunches hasn't sold a picture in a long time, then the agent must defend the expense. Not a pretty picture.

Selling

A good agent knows what the Hollywood community wants to buy at any particular moment. Since this information can change on a dime it requires a constant flow of give and take with other insiders. This requires great personal relationships with a large number of producers, studio executives, story editors, television show-runners, assistants, and development executives.

Agents also need to have good reputations with these people so that their material gets read quickly and with an open mind. Agents have to know how to close a deal, get the material to the right people, get buzz going around town about their hot new spec script, and, often, they must have the ability to package a project with the right director, star, and producer. As we've discussed, packaging in and of itself is very complex and certain agents in the large agencies specialize in this arena. All of the above takes a great deal of savvy and know-how.

Selling also requires an agent to build relationships with people who will share information with them. Agents need people to give them private phone numbers and email addresses of important players, as well as information that may have been told to them in private.

I've always felt that selling is really about hope. An agent can only present your work and then hope that someone will buy it. An agent must know the entertainment business inside and out to try and find the right script for the right buyer; that's a big part of what makes him or her a good agent.

BIG OR SMALL?

Once you understand the basic work of your agent you also need to know the huge differences between large and small agencies. Let's start with the larger agencies. ICM, William Morris Endeavor, CAA, APA, and so on, are big and have many agents, employees, department heads, lawyers, accountants, administrators, human resources personnel, in-house readers (story department), and various talent departments such as actors, music, literary, and more. All of this seems well and good until you realize that this means that your agent must go to endless meetings and be subject to the pressures of inside as well as outside competition. These agents are also under the pressure of doing what they are told by their department heads and the heads of the agency itself. However, they do have those helpful legal and accounting departments to work with them on negotiating deals and reviewing complicated contracts.

Agents who work for a small agency (sometimes known as "boutique" agencies) must handle all of the aforementioned responsiblities and additionally deal with some of the tasks that a large agency would be able to give to their various departments. Without these extra hands the agents at the smaller companies must do all of the work themselves, which adds countless hours to an already long day. The smaller companies have a certain amount of freedom and may be better able to juggle their time to better service their clients more personally and with more thought. They are usually run by people with an entrepreneurial spirit and a creative bent. In a large agency clients are more likely to speak to the assistants on a regular basis than with their own agents. In the smaller agencies you will be more likely to have a real relationship and direct connection with your agent.

A DAY IN THE LIFE OF AN AGENT

What I loved most about working as an agent was the constant changes in my work on an hourly or sometimes even on a minute-by-minute basis. Every day there were new situations I had to deal with and resolve. Client emergencies and/or needs came up that I had to tend to immediately. Surprises happened all of the time.

Each day I would begin with a review of my "call sheet." I would carry over any calls that weren't dealt with on the previous day and then I'd add new people to call for the "today" list. I remember checking my client list to see if there was anything new that I could do for each client each day. Perhaps I would send out a sample of a client's writing if I'd made a new contact, or remind a client to hustle a bit more on her latest spec script or treatment. When I would read in the trades about new development executives being hired, I would make cold calls to them and try to set up lunch or breakfast dates. My call sheet could begin with about fifty calls and by the end of the day it would be close to one hundred — incoming and outgoing.

Sometimes there was a deal or two that I was negotiating and often the mail brought contracts to be reviewed, new material to peruse, client checks to be processed, query letters, and more. Each bit of mail required some form of my attention. Since I owned a boutique-sized agency I did a great deal of the day-to-day work myself. I did not have an accounting department, or a legal department, or a human resources department, nor did I have the luxury of an office administrator. All of these jobs were filled by me and I loved every minute of it. There were always exciting and interesting challenges constantly heading my way.

Working with writers was most gratifying when they met me half-way. I always pushed my clients to be working on new projects, on spec, if they were not currently under contract on a studio or network project. I also wanted them to keep in touch with all of their past and present connections. Networking is a job that never stops for either the client or the agent. Years ago I heard an agent friend of mine, Jim Gibson, say: "My clients get to keep ninety percent of the money, so they should do ninety percent of the work." That may be a funny line but there is also a ring of truth to it. Some clients hate writing new screenplays so they spend lots of time calling their agent to prod them into getting them jobs. The system doesn't work that way. It takes two to make it happen.

A former client of mine, Ronnie Christensen, used to say, "I wouldn't even think about sending out my troops without ammunition." He was always coming up with new specs and new ideas. Prolific clients are great if their material is great. Some writers work too fast and present poor work. This is a bad habit. You must always work in a professional manner and present your writing efforts in the best possible light.

On weekends I would sometimes review contracts at home and there was always more reading to be done. Some weekends I would put together a business dinner party or go out with clients and their spouses.

I hope this helps when you are frustrated and wondering what your agent is doing when he or she is not returning your phone calls.

> **EXERCISES**

1. Research four Los Angeles theatrical and/or literary agencies.

2. Check with the WGA and find an agency that will look at new writers' material.

3. Analyze your projects to see if they are marketable, i.e., work falling into genres that sell to a wide audience like thrillers, teen comedies, and contemporary action-adventure.

4. Start sending out those query letters.

5. Check the Internet to see if any agents are speaking in your area.

THE WHOLE BALL OF WAX: AGENTS, PERSONAL MANAGERS, BUSINESS MANAGERS, AND LAWYERS

16

It seems there are specialists in every field. The entertainment industry is no different. You will need people who really know the ins and outs of our particular business to help guide you through the complex practical and financial aspects of a writing career. You need to get your material read, deals negotiated, contracts reviewed, money handled, business decisions made, and choices determined. These are some of the reasons that agents, personal managers, business managers, and lawyers abound.

AGENTS AND MANAGERS

If you are a new writer you don't need a huge support system but you definitely need an agent and/or a personal manager. Once you have completed at least two or three really good screenplays or TV sample scripts, you should try to secure the services of a personal manager or agent. If you get a personal manager, his or her job is to find an agent for you. This is a major undertaking and your manager must have a strong belief in your abilities and talents. Once your manager finds an agent for you it is usually a gross error to fire that manager.

Your manager has procured representation for you and now will work with you creatively on your scripts. This includes deciding which story idea to pursue next and consulting with you on making the project better. The manager also prods the agent to get your material read by the right people and to set up "meet & greet" meetings for you so that you develop relationships in the industry.

A personal manager watches over your career and keeps you everpresent in the mind and work of your agency. Personal managers are not allowed to seek employment or negotiate deals for their writer clients. Unlike agencies, they are not licensed by the state of California. They also do not have to sign an agreement with the Writers Guild of America, as agents do. They usually have a much smaller client list than most agencies and so they can spend more time and energy on you than your agent. In too many instances a writer and his or her agency representative do not fit together very well. In that event it's great to have a personal manager who knows you and has a track record with you. The manager may have to go back to the drawing board and find you a new agent.

I once had a very odd situation with a client who had become an extremely successful feature film writer during the time I was his agent. He made tons of money and all the head honchos in town sought him out. For some strange reason he decided to leave my agency and to sign with a different agency. After he left me his career did a very deep nose-dive and he stopped working. His new agency mishandled his career terribly. Naturally he called me and asked to come back as a client. I took him back. During that time I decided to change from working as an agent to becoming a personal manager. The client stayed with me and I began to search for an agent for him. Because he had harmed his career by leaving me and moved to a poor choice of agents, he was now a very cold commodity in the film market. I was unable to find an agent for him. I did secure a writing assignment for him on a miniseries. Without an agent and because I had been his agent for quite some time, I went ahead and negotiated his deal and then had his attorney finish the negotiations to hone the fine points of the contract. Now that he had a great job, the client left me once again. He was able to get out of his contract with me because I had negotiated his deal. This was a very unpleasant and unhappy situation for me because I had always believed in this young writer and had fought for him all the way.

Personal managers usually take between 10% and 15% of your gross earnings. These fees are sometimes negotiable, but once they are set… they are set in stone. Additionally, personal managers often include themselves as producers on their clients' projects. Agents cannot do this.

Sample Contract: Personal Manager – Writer

MANAGEMENT CONTRACT

March 1, 2010

Ms. Michele Wallerstein
Wallerstein Management
4314 Jones Street, Ste. 104
Los Angeles, CA 99999

Dear Michele:

This letter will set forth our agreement as follows:

1. ENGAGEMENT & TERM: I,_____
(Artist) desire to obtain your advice, counsel and direction in the development of my professional career. In view of the foregoing, I hereby engage you (Manager) as my sole and exclusive personal manager in the writing, producing, and literary fields, throughout the world, for the term of two (2) years, commencing today, March 1, 2010, under the terms and conditions herein set forth.

2. SERVICES: Manager agrees to perform one or more of these services: advise and counsel on all work-related matters; advise and counsel in any and all matters pertaining to public relations; advise and counsel with relation to the adoption of proper formats for presentation of talents of Artist and in the determination of proper style, business and characterization in keeping with those talents; advise and counsel with regard

to general practices in the entertainment industry and with respect to such matters of which Manager may have knowledge concerning compensation and privileges extended for similar artistic values; advise and counsel Artist concerning the selection of talent agencies, persons, firms and corporations who will counsel, advise, seek, and procure employment and engagements for Artist, and supervise the services of such persons, firms and corporations with respect to Artists; to supervise the negotiating of the terms of Artist's contracts; and generally to exert itself in Artist's best interest and to Artist's profit, benefit, and advantage in all branches of the entertainment field.

3. COMPENSATION:

(A) Artist agrees to pay to Manager a sum equal to ten percent (10%) of any and all monies or other compensations which I earn and actually receive during the term hereof or anytime after the expiration of this Agreement if I am entitled to receive the same on account of or pursuant to any contract that has been entered into or has been substantially negotiated during the term of this Agreement.

The commission(s) set forth above shall be based on the gross monies or other considerations that I earn and receive from all applicable engagements, contracts, and agreements pursuant to the terms set forth in said engagements, contracts, and agreements or agreed upon prior to the expiration of the term hereof including all renewals and extensions of any agreement entered into during the term hereof even though such renewal and/ or extension of option exercise for such extension shall occur after the term hereof. Consistent with the foregoing, you shall not commission any additional gross monies or other considerations that I earn and receive from improved terms of such engagements, contracts, and agreements if such improved terms are agreed upon subsequent to the expiration of the term hereof.

(B) Your percentage share shall extend to all gross monies or other considerations (excluding actual attorney's fees), which I actually receive from judgments, awards, settlements, payments, and proceeds related to or arising out of a breach by the contracting party (or parties) of any engagement, contract, or agreement which is "entered into" during the term of this Agreement.

4. NON EXCLUSIVITY and PRODUCING SERVICES:

(A) Your services are non-exclusive and you shall at all times be free to perform the same or similar services for other writers, as well as to engage in any and all other business activities, including, without limitation, feature film and television production.

(B) I understand and agree that Manager may package or act as the entrepreneur or promoter of any entertainment program in which I am engaged, or may produce or co-produce entertainment projects with me or utilizing my literary work. Such activity on Manager's part shall not constitute a breach of this Agreement or of Manager's fiduciary obligations and duties to me.

ACCEPTED AND AGREED TO:
WALLERSTEIN MANAGEMENT, INC.
By:_____
Michele Wallerstein

ACCEPTED AND AGREED TO:

By: (Artist) _____

Date: _____

Sample Contract: Agency – Writer

Below is a copy of a standard agency/writer contract. The WGA Rider W is an attachment to all agency contracts to further protect writers and their rights. You can call the WGA in Los Angeles or New York to procure a copy of the Rider W.

ABCD & Associates
A Talent and Literary Agency
60000 Wilshire Blvd., Suite 100
Los Angeles, CA 99999

_____

(Date)

Re: General Service Agreement

Dear_____:
  (Owner)

    1. I hereby employ you as my sole and exclusive agent, personal representative, artist's manager, and advisor for a period of <u>2</u> years, commencing on the date hereof, to negotiate contracts and agreements for (a) the rendition of my services (hereinafter sometimes called "professional services") as a writer, artist, director, producer, or any similar capacity in the field of entertainment and in the literary fields; (b) the sale, lease, license, assignment or other disposition of any literary or dramatic material of any package, as the term "package" is hereafter defined (or any rights in any of the foregoing), acquired, created, owned or controlled in whole or in part by me or any corporation, partnership, firm or other entity owned or controlled in whole or in part, or in which I have an interest, either directly or indirectly; and (c) advertising and commercial tie-ups using my name, voice or likeness.

The Labor Commissioner has no jurisdiction over "Materials and Packages" agreements and therefore, neither approves nor disapproves the provision of this Agreement that pertain or apply hereto.

2. You accept this employment. You agree to use reasonable efforts to procure employment and to negotiate and otherwise act for me as aforesaid. You further agree to advise and counsel me in the development and advancement of my professional career.

3. As consideration for your said services to be rendered hereunder, I agree to pay you and you shall be entitled to receive a sum equal to ten percent (10%) of the gross compensation earned or received by me directly or indirectly for, from, or in connection with the sale, license, assignment or other disposition of any such literary or dramatic material or any such packages (or any rights in any of the foregoing); the rendition of my professional services; and any form of advertising or commercial tie-ups, using my name, voice, or likeness.

"Gross Compensation" as used herein is defined to include, but is not limited to, all monies, salaries, earnings, fees, royalties, bonuses, shares of profit, and other things of value without deductions of any kind, earned or received by me directly or indirectly for, from, under, or in connection with (a) contracts or agreements for the sale, lease, license, assignment or other disposition of any literary or dramatic material or any such packages (or any rights in the foregoing, or for the rendition of any professional services or for any such advertising or commercial tie-ups, whether such contracts or agreements are now in existence or are negotiated for or entered into during the term herein; and (b) immediate or future extensions, renewals, substitutions, or replacements (whether any of the foregoing be upon the same or different terms) of any such contracts or agreements.

The payments to be made to you hereunder shall be payable to you or your assigns within fifteen (15) days of receipts, directly or indirectly by me, my heirs, next of kin, executors, administrators, assigns, or on my behalf (whichever first occurs), of the compensation involved; and regardless of whether or not such contracts or agreements, extensions, renewals, substitutions or replacements were procured by you, by me, or by or through any third person, firm or corporation; and regardless of whether or not the term of any such contract, agreement, extension, renewal, substitution, or replacement is now in effect or comes into effect during or after the term hereof; and even though the compensation payable under or in connection with any such contract, agreement, extension, renewal, substitution, or replacement may become due or payable after the expiration or prior termination of the term hereof.

4. I hereby agree that you may render your services to others during the term hereof. I hereby warrant, represent, and agree that I am the owner of all rights in and to the material mentioned herein, and that I can dispose thereof; I have not given and will not give anyone else the right or authority to act for me during the term hereof in the capacity in which I have employed you; I am free to enter into this agreement, and neither have nor shall have any contract, agreement, or other obligations which might conflict with any of the provisions of this agreement or interfere with my obligations hereunder or your rights and benefits hereunder.

5. In the event I do not obtain a bona fide offer for the rendition of my professional services from a responsible employer during a period of three (3) consecutive months, during all of which said time I shall be ready, willing and available to accept such bona fide offer, either party hereto shall have the right to terminate your representation of me under subdivision (a) of paragraph 1 above only by notice, in writing, sent to the other by registered or certified mail, provided no such bona fide offer to be obtained subsequent to the expiration of said three (3) months period and prior to the giving of said notice. No such termination shall affect your right to receive and my obligation to make payments provided for in paragraph 3 hereof, or your right to continue to represent me under subdivisions (b) and (c) of paragraph 1 above.

If, within three (3) months after the end of the term hereof (as extended), I accept any offer on terms similar or reasonably comparable to any offer made to me during the terms hereof (as extended), from or through the same offer, the contract resulting shall be subject to all the terms hereof.

Notwithstanding anything contained in this contract, the term hereof shall continue with respect to any package sold, leased, licensed, assigned, or otherwise disposed of hereunder until one (1) year after the expiration or other termination of any contract or agreement negotiated by you with regard to such package, together with any extensions, renewals, substitutions, or replacements of any such contract or agreement, or until the expiration of this contract, whichever shall be longer.

6. Controversies arising between us under the provisions of the California Labor Code relating to talent agencies and under the rules and regulations for the enforcement thereof, shall be referred to the State Labor Commissioner, as provided in Section 1700-44 of said code, save and except to the extent that the laws of the State of California now or hereafter in force may permit the reference of any such controversy to any other person or group of persons, and save and except to the extent of any controversies arising between us with regard to the sales, lease, license, assignment, or other disposition of the above-mentioned literary or dramatic material or packages (or any rights in any of the foregoing).

7. "Field of entertainment" as used herein includes all phases and future developments of the fields of motion pictures, legitimate stage, musical, radio broadcasting, television, and all other phases and future developments of public or private entertainment.

The terms "contract" and "agreement" as used herein include any extensions, renewals, substitutions, or replacements thereof.

The term "package" as used herein includes any television or radio show, production, program, motion picture, or any series thereof or any reproduction by any present or future process now or ever devised of any of the foregoing in connection with which I produce or furnish or any person, firm partnership, corporation, or other entity in which I have or shall have any interest of any kind shall produce or furnish services or material, or both. If any such literary or dramatic material or any such packages are assigned or transferred by operation of law to any person, partnership, firm, corporation, or other entity, or are assigned or transferred by me to any person, partnership, firm, corporation, or other entity in which I have any interest, either directly or indirectly, such assignment or transfer shall be subject to all of your rights hereunder. I agree to notify you in writing of any such assignment or transfer prior to the effect thereof and to require the assignee or transferee to assume, in writing, my obligation to you hereunder.

8. You may assign this agreement to any corporation, partnership, or other firm with which you join or which results from the reorganization, consolidation, or merger of your agency business or your artists' management business, with Artist's approval and the approval of the State Labor Commissioner. Should any provision of this agreement be void or unenforceable, such provision shall be deemed omitted only to the extent necessary to make this agreement valid and enforceable, and this agreement with such provision as so omitted shall remain in full force and effect. This instrument sets forth the entire agreement between us. It shall not become effective until accepted and executed by you. As an inducement to you to execute this agreement, I represent and warrant that no statement, promise, representation, or inducement except as herein set forth has been made on your behalf or by any of your employees or representatives. This agreement may not be canceled, altered, or amended, except by an instrument in writing signed by you and me.

Very truly yours,

_____

Artist

Accepted and Agreed to by:

_____

Agency

This Talent Agency is licensed by the Labor Commissioner of the State of California. This form of contract has been approved by the State Labor Commissioner.

BUSINESS MANAGERS AND LAWYERS

The time to hire business managers and accountants is clearly when there is so much money coming in that you don't know how to do your own taxes anymore or where to put all that cash. These professionals can advise you about buying that condo or setting up an IRA, or forming a corporation. These advisors usually charge 5% of 100% of all of a writer's gross earnings.

Your agent or manager may help you find a good lawyer. Of course there are many great attorneys who know the business inside and out and who will do a great job for their clients. They will go over your contracts to make sure that everything is legal and in place. They often come up with good ideas for changes in your contracts and will fight for them for you. Lawyers sometimes send out your scripts if you don't have an agent. Most people hesitate before agreeing to read something that's been sent over by a lawyer, whose training is in law and business, not in creative writing. Attorneys charge by the hour; some of them will also charge a percentage of your gross income.

EVALUATING YOUR REPRESENTATIVES

You can tell if your representatives are good if they are getting their jobs done. Ask yourself the following questions:

a. Is your agent submitting your material? Is he or she setting up meetings for you? Is he or she negotiating proper deals for you? Does your agent (or your agent's assistants) return your calls in a timely manner?

b. Is your attorney finding problems in your contracts and resolving those issues satisfactorily? Is he or she working with alacrity?

c. Does your manager speak with you and with your agent often? Does he or she have good connections in the business and good ideas for your work?

d. Are your business managers taking good care of your future? Do they make good decisions for you? Do you always know exactly how much money you have and where it is?

Never forget that you are in charge of your life. All the final decisions come down to you and you must make informed choices. It's great to trust your reps but never close your eyes to what is going on in your business life.

> EXERCISES

1. Thoroughly read the management and artist contracts and note that they are in the form of letters from the artist who is hiring the manager and/or agent.

2. Note the provisions for the manager to act as a producer during his or her tenure as a manager.

3. Note the three month "out clause" in Paragraph 5 of the agency contract.

HOW TO GET, KEEP, AND WHEN TO FIRE AN AGENT

17

It's always been interesting to me to see the variations in the agent-client relationship. Naturally, in the beginning a new writer wants desperately to get an agent but has little to offer. Conversely, agents want desperately to sign writers who have already sold, make lots of money and have great reputations. For you to overcome this crevasse is both difficult and tricky.

LANDING AN AGENT

The entertainment business is a business, and the same laws apply as they do in any business. This means "the law of supply and demand." You supply the world with great scripts and there will be agents lined up to sign you. This is mostly true. Really good writers get found wherever they are unless those writers are totally self-destructive and never let anyone read their work and hide their scripts in a closet. There are lots of other self-destructive habits that can ruin a career before it begins. A bad attitude will hurt you every time. Fear of rejection is a real problem. The list goes on and on.

However, if you are reasonably sane you will eventually be read and thus you will be discovered. Remember that everyone in Hollywood is always looking for the next great writer. It only seems as if they are not. Please notice all the industry professionals who miraculously appear at seminars, film festivals, writer's conferences, etc. They come, or were sent by their bosses, to find you. If you are as great as you think you are then these people will get promotions and raises and bonuses for finding you. They can't get to the top without you.

Another great way to be considered is via referrals. Try other writers, or friends, or writing teachers or consultants. You will probably have to push for these referrals. Promise your first born if necessary, but get someone to make a call on your behalf. Agents always look at referred material before anything else. This is where you need to be networking with other writers, joining writers' groups, and taking seminars where you can interact with other writers who may now have or in the future may have an agent who could be a good fit for you.

All of the above will only work if your manuscript is wonderful. Make sure that your story is solid, your characters are real and believable, and your plot is interesting; and don't forget that grammar and spelling always count.

Once an agent reads your work and likes it he or she should set up a meeting with you. It's a doozy because your first chance to connect with this person may be the only one you get. Be sure you get there early, dress cleanly, listen well, and share things about yourself and your work. If you don't speak, you won't be remembered. These initial meetings rarely last over one hour. If you are there longer than that, you might be overstaying your welcome.

Any good agent will want to read two or three other spec scripts you've written, preferably in the same genre. Make sure you have those back-up pieces ready to go. This is the most important aspect of finding an agent who will want to sign you. As an agent I never read a writer's first script and I would never read a potential client who only had two good scripts. It is a body of work that will inspire an agent to sign you more than anything else. We want to know that you will work on your career at least as hard as we do.

On a rare occasion an agent will decide to keep you as a "hip-pocket" client. That means that you will not sign agency contracts, but the agent is there for you if you need him or her. This sometimes happens if you are referred by a friend and need an agent to submit your material to someone who has asked to see it. Perhaps a development person you've met on the tennis court or in the supermarket expressed interest in the idea you mentioned. Most professionals will want to see the material if it is submitted by a bona fide agent. It also gives you a modicum of protection against having your idea stolen or being taken advantage of in some other way. Some people frown on the hip-pocket client routine but I think it's a great way to get your foot in the door. At least you have the ear of an agent if you have some questions, and if you have more material that agent will most likely be predisposed to reading it. If you become a signed client with that agency, then everyone is happy.

BUILDING THE RELATIONSHIP

Okay, now they've read your material, had a couple of meetings with you, and decided to take you on as an agency client. Wow! You have an agent. An interesting bit of information is that when you sign a contract with an agency you are literally hiring them. Everyone feels like it's the other way around and most agencies also behave that way. Try to keep in mind that the agent works for you, that you are a team, and that you need each other. It's up to you to make him or her a really good agent for you and to keep this relationship a positive and productive one. The reality of the relationship is that the agent is pretty much the boss. You are depending on his or her expertise and know-how. They know the right people and can get you into places that you would never be able to enter alone. They can get you meetings with famous producers and hungry development execs. Your job is to be constantly coming up with new story ideas and new scripts. It is not your job to come up with producers or studios that you think will like your film. Your agent will know this better than you do. If you keep supplying your agent with terrific new material, then you may call him or her once a week. It is also a good idea to always be prepared to pitch new ideas just in case your agent gets spur-of-the-moment pitch meetings for you.

As a rule it's a good idea to call your agent on Tuesdays, which will give them almost a week to put more energy into you and your work. Mondays are tough because they all have staff meetings and end up running late the rest of the day. The worst thing you can do vis-a-vis your relationship is to be defensive and belligerent. No one wants to take the call of a "pain in the ass." Whining is also up there in the Top Ten list of things not to do. Lots of product and a positive and professional attitude are your greatest assets. Remember that you and your agent are a team. You are both on the same side.

The teamwork aspect of your relationship should work both ways. You also have a right to ask questions and get answers.

SHOULD I MOVE ON?

Now let's say that everything has gone well for a year or two. Perhaps you've sold a script, been hired for a rewrite or two, had lots of meetings and made more good, solid contacts via your agent. Your agent seems to like you and believes in you and your work. But, people start to tell you about a better agent or a bigger agency or that your last deal wasn't big enough. This begins to nag at you. Maybe your agent didn't return your last call in a timely way, or didn't like your last two scripts, or didn't get you read by the president of a studio. Are these fair complaints? What now?

Stop and think. Try to be fair in your judgment. Ask yourself these very important questions about yourself as a client before you fire that agent and go elsewhere:

a. How good were your last two scripts? Where they really marketable, well written, competitive?

b. Have you been calling the agent every day or two? Are you hounding him or her without a good reason?

c. Do you easily give in to peer pressure?

d. Are you in a state of panic because of financial pressures at home?

e. Has your work been well received by the buying community?

f. Have you come up with new ideas and pitched them to your agent?

g. Have your meetings gone well with buyers? Were you on time? Did you have a positive attitude? Did you try to bring fresh ideas?

The answers to these questions will help you to know whether you have been the right kind of client or whether you simply want to blame someone else for any problems you may be having in your career. It is up to you to take responsibility for your own actions and your own culpability in the relationship.

If you continue to be tempted to leave your agent and you have explored all of these questions, ask yourself the following questions about the agent's work:

    a. Is your agent honest with you?
    b. Does your agent have a good reputation?
    c. Is your agent responsive to your work and your phone calls?
    d. Does your agent give you good advice?
    e. Is your agent getting you and/or your work out into the buying community?
    f. Is your agent negotiating well on your behalf?

Now, sit back and take a breath and remember the golden rule of the agent-client relationship: "If it ain't broke, don't fix it."

Over the years I've witnessed so many writers shoot themselves in the foot by leaving good agents who believed in them.

When you change agencies, your writing career is put on hold for quite a long time. Invariably you will lose good connections with people who like your agency and don't like that you've fired them. There is a long lag time between firing your agency and signing up with the new agency where you have to meet with everyone there and push to see that they all read your work (which they won't). It will take additional time for you to try to figure out who your real contact in the agency is and to make sure that the assistants like you too. All of this can take months. If there is "heat" on you, any time lost will never be regained, and you may fall off of the "hot list" that you and your previous agent worked so hard to create.

The new agency will have wooed you because you have already made money and they want the "easy" sales. You become one more on their never-ending list of clients, another notch on their belt.

Another essential before changing agents is to see if there is a problem in your career that lies within you. This is of paramount importance. Ask yourself if you are pitching the same (or similar) old ideas. Have you given your agent a new and excellent screenplay? Without ammunition, an agent cannot do the impossible. Be very sure to take responsibility and to acknowledge to yourself that you are the one in charge of your own career.

It's never a good idea to turn all of your personal power over to someone else. You don't want to be totally dependent on your agent. The following story is an example of how dependent some clients feel.

Years ago I had to go into the hospital for a few days for some minor surgery. I called my clients to let them know. One client, who was a TV comedy writer, exclaimed, "Oh, my God, what will I do?" He was a grown man with a wife, a lawyer, and two grown daughters. Now that was the definition of someone who is much too dependent on his agent. I did find out, some years later, that he had a bad drug problem.

Don't react to outside pressure. The loss to you and your work life cannot be regained. As in any other relationship, try your best to make this one work. Have a meeting with your agent to discuss any concerns you might have. Listen to what your agent has to say.

Sometimes agents do go cold on some of their clients. It is almost always because the client has stopped writing, or is turning in poor work. I've noticed a rather strange phenomenon with agents that seems to be true no matter whom they are representing: Agents hate to fire clients. It's just an odd fact of life. What agents will do is stop returning your calls, stop sending out your material, stop pitching you for writing assignments, etc. This is why you must be vigilant and find out what your agent is doing about your career at all times. It is also the reason you must keep bringing new ideas to the table.

As long as your agent has been honest with you, worked on your material, responded to your calls, and made good deals for you, stay where you are and put your time, energy, and concentration into your writing.

Prior to leaving the agency business I represented a bright, young, new and talented writer. We had a great working relationship. I taught him everything about the business, sent out his wonderful spec script, and within a month of signing him I negotiated a sale price of $750,000 for that screenplay! We sold more of his screenplays at that price and I was able to get writing assignments for him with huge paydays. After a couple of great years together, I suddenly received a phone call from him telling me that he was leaving my agency and going with someone else. I had no idea that anything like this was on his mind or that we had any problems whatsoever. So, he left. Within months his career ended with a whimper. He had made a poor choice and was no longer thought of as the hot young writer in Hollywood. Once a writer falls off the "hot list" there is no climbing back on. The wild ride is over. Reputation is everything and once it is hurt, no major player will take a chance on that writer, or actor, or director, etc. I advise you to remember that saying I mentioned previously: "If it ain't broke, don't fix it."

> EXERCISES

1. Find professional writers via the Internet and ask them about their agents.

2. Call past and present writing teachers and ask for agent contacts.

3. Check with other writers about their agency experiences.

4. Call people to see if anyone can refer you to an agent.

5. Do not sign with any agent who lives outside of the greater Los Angeles area or has a second job!

THE TEN RULES TO A GREAT
AGENT-CLIENT RELATIONSHIP

18

New and even experienced writers often have an unrealistic view of what their agents should be like, as well as what their agents can and will do for them. In the movie *Jerry Maguire*, Tom Cruise was always there for the Cuba Gooding, Jr. character. Cruise had dinner with Gooding's family, he went to all of his games, he was constantly on the phone with him and he even carried his bags. Not a chance!

Your agent is not going to be your best friend. He or she is not going to hold your hand, listen to your personal problems, take all of your calls, meet you for coffee every morning, or really care if your dog dies. Agents don't have time. It's not their job, and, if they did all of these things for all of their clients, they would be lousy agents!

Let's face it, you really don't need those hand-holding jobs to be filled by an agent, do you? Get a friend or spouse to fulfill those needs. "Show business" is business and you must treat it as such. Having a friendly relationship with your agent is fine. I always worked with clients who I liked as people as well as liking their work as artists. You don't want to try to give orders to your agent, or be belligerent with him or her, and you don't want him or her to be rude to you. What you do want, and have a right to expect, is a mutually friendly and respectful quid pro quo. Make a note that agents have a very limited amount of time in their daily lives. They work a million hours per day, twenty days a week. Keep in mind that when your agent is on the phone with you or emailing you, then he or she is not on the phone or emailing buyers for you!

TEN RULES FOR MAINTAINING A GREAT RELATIONSHIP WITH YOUR AGENT

1. What you should expect from your agent is a reasonable amount of communication. This means a response to your email if you ask a real and specific question on an occasional basis. If you have questions every day, save them up and send a list once a week. If possible, send them to the assistant. Don't be a nag or a pest to your agent. You are entitled to know where and when your material has been sent.

I was often asked by clients why their material was turned down by this or that production company. My usual answer was, "Because they are nuts." I never sent out projects that I did not believe in and, if they were rejected, it was my opinion that the buyer was simply wrong. Agents send screenplays to many producers, who have varying tastes and needs. If you listen to every reason that they have for saying "no," you will drive yourself crazy. It's as simple as accepting the reality that you can't please everyone, so my advice is to just let it go.

2. It is your responsibility to continually bring new ideas, pitches, treatments, and original screenplays to your agent. You should get your agent's input prior to writing the screenplay. Do not blindside your agent with a new script that you have not discussed with him or her. Let your agent know, in advance, what your subject matter is, the basic story, and the genre of your new ideas. As I've mentioned previously, I have had the experience of having clients bring new original screenplays to me that I knew nothing about. This can be a very difficult situation between agent and client if the agent knows that a particular type of project is not of interest to studios at the moment. In that event it is, sadly, a terrible waste of the writer's time and creative energy.

3. Don't expect to get writing assignments if you are not the hottest writer in town. Don't expect to get huge million dollar paydays with each assignment that you do get. Everyone talks about the great writing assignments they are up for or or the ones their writer-colleagues just finished (but they themselves almost got), or the jobs their agents promised to get for them. For the most part this is a fantasy. Hollywood lives on gossip and bulls$*t and egos. It's a bad idea to expect your agent to get you rewrite assignments or assignments to adapt a novel for the screen if you are not one of the biggest A-list writers in town. The chances of getting writing assignments are small but possible. Sometimes you might meet with a production company because they loved your original script and they are looking for someone to rewrite a similar project. It's possible to get this type of assignment when you are fairly new, if you come up with some great ideas for their project that no one else has had. The company may not be able to afford an A-lister, but they can afford you.

Be realistic in your demands on your agent. Most of the time production companies that have studio backing on a project will go to major writers with lots of experience, and pay them huge amounts. Small movies with small budgets might take a chance on a newer writer for a smaller fee. A new writer must have at least three terrific spec scripts in the same genre as the movie that needs a fresh writer. You need to trust your agent to know what offers you should or should not take. If the offer is low but the project has the potential of leading to better assignments, the agent may want you to accept it to enhance your future career. That's the way things work.

4. If you've been getting writing assignments and they stop coming, don't blame your agent. First look to yourself. You may have been "cooling off" around town. You may not have been listening to the notes you've been given by the producers or their development people. You may be too demanding or too slow with the work. Perhaps you've been showing up to development meetings late, or you've been poorly prepared when you get there. You may be too argumentative with the people who are giving you notes. Watch that attitude. You can't expect an agent to resurrect a ruined career. If you have a good reputation you will probably continue to work.

5. You must trust your agent when it comes to negotiating for you. Negotiations are very complicated and many elements come into play that you know nothing about. Perhaps the buyers are also interested in another project similar to yours and are using that as a tactic to keep the price low, or they are close to the end of their fiscal year when they are negotiating on your behalf. Remember that the better the deal is for you, the better the commission is for them. Your agent may know that this is the only game in town for your script. Let your agent do his or her job… and you do yours.

I once represented a very good TV writer who was offered a staff job on a sitcom. "John" needed the work and we were happy to get this long-term assignment. After I had closed the deal with John's blessing, he thought about it some more and came back to me insisting that I go back to the negotiators and get additional monies. I argued with him because I know that once you close a deal it stays closed. Because he demanded that I do it, I did go back to those people. Neither John nor I ever worked for or with that producer again. He put me in a very bad position with buyers and I could never find it in my heart or my head to forget it.

6. Don't expect your agent to continue sending out your old scripts forever. Once they've been out to the town they get cold. They may continue to be used as writing samples for particular projects, but not as saleable scripts. Hollywood is a small town and everyone knows about every script. Always be ready with new ideas and screenplays.

7. Remember, when it comes to making a success of your career, no one is more on your side than your agent. If you make money, so does your agent – the person who has spent time and money on you without any guarantees. Agents are the ones who make the first investment. Always think of them as teammates who are working with you toward a common goal. Let them know that you are aware of the work they are doing for you.

8. You should expect your agent to read your work, take some of your calls, get your work out to mainstream production companies, share information with you, be actively and creatively involved in your writing career, and help you become a better client.

9. You need to spend your time being supportive of your agent, and doing your share of the work making yourself a successful writer. Constantly work on coming up with new ideas, new screenplays, and new contacts. Hone your craft. Be willing to improve your work and be patient.

10. Being fair in any relationship works both ways. Agents sign both new and professional writers to improve, manage, and tend to their careers. You want your agent to be fair with you but you must remember to be fair with him or her. Agents introduce writers to the buying community in Hollywood via your work. They take out your material and submit it to many buyers in hopes of selling the script itself or perhaps getting a writing assignment for you. The very least they hope for is to get you a meeting with these people as a precursor to a future working relationship. They do all of these things without getting paid, without any guarantees, and with a great deal of hope. Many times, a client will secure a job on his or her own, or through a friend or previous employer. Does the agent deserve that client's commission? You bet!

I have met with many creative people over the years who had varying degrees of success. They were interested in changing agents and we would meet to discuss the possibility of my taking them on as clients.

In a couple of these cases the potential clients were television series directors who wanted to move into the TV movie or feature film arenas. One of these was a director and former actor — I'll call him Jimmy. I'd always admired his work and was thrilled to meet him. He had great TV series credits and wanted to get into directing TV movies. We had lunch at a café on Sunset Boulevard and a couple of meetings in my office. We were close to deciding to work together when he announced that he often worked for an executive producer who had an overall deal at that time with Stephen J. Cannell, and that if this particular producer called him to direct any of his shows, Jimmy did not want to pay commissions on those episodes. That meant that if I was able to get him the TV movie assignment and if he had scheduled an episode for that producer, then he wouldn't be available and I would have worked for nothing. I couldn't work with him under those conditions so we parted ways. Like I said before, "Fair works both ways."

●●●

If you understand and carry out all of the above "rules," you will have a long and successful agent-client relationship.

> **EXERCISES**

1.   Practice pitching your screenplay ideas.

2.   Have at least three new ideas ready to pitch.

3.   Write short treatments (three to ten pages) on those pitches.

III GETTING THE BUSINESS

DEALING WITH HOLLYWOOD 19

Selling a screenplay isn't like selling a sack of potatoes. You don't simply hand over your script and receive a big check. All those articles you read in *Variety* and the *Hollywood Reporter* and the stories that people throw around at lunches and parties are hyperbole. Exaggeration is the language of Hollywood. You will read articles in the trade magazines that scream out things like: "*New Writer Sells First Screenplay to Warner Bros for a High 6 Figures.*"

"Wow!" you will say. "Some newbie just got a check for $900,000. This could happen to me." You halfway imagine that the script fell out of the sky and into the hands of an upper-level motion picture studio executive who loved it and wrote a huge check. Well, not so fast, pal. We would all like to think that it happens this way, but it doesn't. The chances of a newbie writer ever seeing that $900,000 payday are slim to none.

The following is the basic scenario as to how a big sale really happens and what those great-sounding numbers in the trades really mean.

THE ANATOMY OF A DEAL

Let's say the writer already had a good agent (and this is saying a lot) who knows the development people at good production companies. He or she loves this latest spec script, which is probably the writer's fifteenth, and sent it to quite a few of these production companies. Let's say the development executive loved the script and gave it to his or her boss, who read the coverage and thought they might be able to sell it to a studio. The boss asked permission (if you're lucky, if not he or she simply snuck it to the studio) from the agent to submit the script to a few studios. The agent said okay, the script was sent, and the writer received no money. This is called a *free option*. Next that wonderful agent spent a few weeks negotiating an *if-come* deal. That means that if a studio wants the project they will have to abide by the deal you agreed upon with the production company that submitted it. Finally it went from the producer to the studio and, lo and behold, the studio liked it.

Now that if-come deal starts to take effect. It was probably a three-page deal memo, drawn up by the agent, that the studio business affairs department made into a fifty-page contract. They will have filled it with lots of additional verbiage that deals with the definition of net profits and how they will make a determination as to whether you will get screen credit and what happens if the script is or is not produced. They will add in what will occur if there is a TV series based on the movie. It will spell out an offered royalty, profit participation in the series, bonuses, etc. All of this is called an *Option/Purchase Agreement*.

If all goes well and the contract is reviewed and agreed upon by the writer, the agent, and the writer's lawyer, it will be signed.

Now, let's say that the producers were successful and a studio decided to develop the screenplay in the hopes of producing a motion picture based on this original work. At this point the writer receives the *option fee*, which is probably about $5,000. Out of that amount the writer has paid his or her attorney many hundreds of dollars and has paid the agent $500 (10% of the option fee), and has paid the IRS another big slice.

Next, the writer had numerous meetings with studio execs and the people from the original production company about their notes as to how the writer needed to change this wonderful screenplay that everyone loved. He or she will then write the first rewrite of the script, for which he or she will be paid a small percentage of that $900,000 purchase price of the script. The first rewrite is often in the amount of the Writers Guild of America's scale price plus 10%, for the agent.

The next steps of the deal are a second rewrite and a polish with defined payments. These steps are not guaranteed to the original writer. The producer and studio may hire any other writer or writers they wish to finish the script. This situation may go on for years. The big "purchase price" of the script is only paid after all other payments to the original writer are deducted and only if the picture is produced. Major motion picture producers and studios almost always bring in one or more of their favorite writers for the rewrites. If those other writers receive any *on-screen credit*, the original writer's *production bonus* drops by the amount paid to those other writers. Production bonuses are a very large fraction of that $900,000 price touted in the trades. This amount is only paid if and when the film is made and if there are no other writers who receive credit. As you can see, that $900,000 may end up to somewhere around $50,000.

Option periods vary in length from approximately six months to two years and the option holder (producer) has the right to extend them for equal or lesser time periods. These time periods are all negotiated via your agent. Renewing the option is up to the producer or studio. If you have a six-month or perhaps a one-year option the production company has the right to drop the project after the initial option period has expired. By that time the material is usually considered old by industry standards.

Your project may lie fallow for a very long time. The option renewal is in the hands of the producer and studio only. You have no choice in this matter.

Be reminded that your agent works for you. Your agent cannot make or accept a deal without getting your okay on it first. Your agent has an obligation to present the offer to you and to make sure that you understand it and all of its ramifications. There will be lots of terms that you don't quite understand and you should ask exactly what they mean. No one expects you to be blessed with an innate ability to comprehend legalese or deal-making lingo in any field.

The Writers Guild of America is also available to you and should be used accordingly. They have a legal department and you may call them at any time to ask questions about your deal and your negotiations. The WGA has certain protections already in place that the producers must adhere to in their contracts with you whether you are a WGA member or not. Both your agent and the production company must be signatories of the *WGA Minimum Basic Agreement*. Because those companies have signed this agreement with the WGA, they cannot pay you less than the WGA-established minimum amounts for your work. You have a right to call them and get a copy of that agreement even if you are not a member.

Your contract on a movie deal will have a net profits paragraph along with a very confusing definition of those net profits. The reality is that they don't really exist. I had the good fortune to represent Bootsie, one of the co-writers of a picture released in 1997 titled *Booty Call*, starring Jamie Foxx, Tommy Davidson, and Vivica A. Fox. I am happy to say that the writers were paid $850,000 for the script. The production cost of the film was roughly $8 million. It made a ton of money in the U.S. and has been shown around the world and released on television, on On Demand, Netflix, etc., yet my client has never received one dime of *net profits*. There are no real profits in "net profits". This provision in your contract has little or no value. A "gross profits definition" is only given to a couple of very, very successful writers, if any. Huge movie stars may get a piece of the gross, but the industry changes so often that that may change too. If you can get a net profit definition that is the same as the movie's leads or producers, you may see some money, but it's not likely.

The lack of net profits is why so many agents do their best to secure the largest sum of money that they can for the up-front payments for their clients. It's more than likely this will be all the money they will ever get.

There are many more important points in an Option/Purchase Agreement, but you must find an agent who is trustworthy and will communicate openly with you. An agent has a contractual responsibility to present all offers to you, and is prohibited from turning down an offer without your knowledge.

The above are classic points that are misunderstood by novices. Agents can also be very creative in negotiating on your behalf. Sometimes they may not win a point in their negotiations that you both may have wanted, but in a trade-off they may be able to wrangle something for you that you didn't even expect.

What I want you to know is that you can't believe everything you hear and read about in the Hollywood community. Of course some of the hype is true, but only about 10% of it. The rest of the stories that you hear and read are only partially true. These great stories will make you crazy with jealousy and envy. Try not to let that happen by remembering that this is a business of blowing everything out of proportion.

Everyone wants to make that big splash and wants the show business world to think that he or she is the hot new commodity of the day. Agents must make their buyers think that they are representing the best new writers. It's the producers' job to let everyone know that they have the hottest new script. It's the studio's job to let the Hollywood community know that they have the best new project. It doesn't really matter to them if they do or not. The game is called "mine is bigger than yours." They play this game every single day of their lives. You become a pawn in it. If you fall for their game it can paralyze you and push you into making bad decisions.

Remember, each person you deal with in this industry has his or her own agenda. Very rarely will you have someone who is on your side for purely altruistic reasons. Finding an ally whose agenda is the same as yours is all the better for both of you. Hopefully that ally is your agent.

Most new writers are terrified of trusting their agents, particularly when it comes to negotiating their first deals. You will probably want to know about every phone conversation, letter, memo, and email that travels between your agent and the deal negotiators. If you insist on this you will drive your agent crazy.

WHAT TO DO (AND NOT TO DO) DURING NEGOTIATIONS

Never force your agent to go back after a deal is agreed upon and ask for something more. This is never well received. Once a deal is closed, it's closed. I once represented a very good writer who forced me into this position after I had made a deal for him to be a producer on a TV sitcom. The executive producer on the show was unhappy with the writer for the balance of his contract and that executive producer would never work with my client or me again.

You must show your agent that you are tough. That means being able to back your agent up if he or she suggests that you turn down the offer. You cannot negotiate well if your client is begging you to take whatever is tendered. You will be cutting him or her off at the knees and you will both lose. An agent needs your ability to trust in his or her judgment and stand firmly with him or her.

One of the biggest points to understand is that you are trying to build a career as a writer, not simply sell or option one script. These movie spec sales will lead to many great things for you. The fact that you have sold a script will open doors for your agent to get you meetings with terrific players and perhaps these people will have rewrite assignments that need a writer with your ability to write great characters, or build a better structure, or describe better action sequences than the original writer. Now you will become that rewrite person who gets to make more and more money and really become a professional, working Hollywood writer.

Not every deal gets made. There are those rare times that you must walk away. Some offers are really terrible and should be passed up. It doesn't happen often and when it does it is extremely difficult for everyone involved. Be prepared for this happenstance.

Hollywood pays writers a great deal of money. The minimums that are established by the Writers Guild of America are very respectable, and very few producers expect to pay only the minimum. If your agent is negotiating for a low-budget film that is a signatory of the WGA agreement, the company will most likely pay at least the minimum fee plus an additional 10%. This 10% is so that you will not receive less than the minimum after your agent receives his or her 10% commission.

Try to remember that if you write two episodes of *Law & Order* it will take you about twelve weeks and you will make more money than most Americans earn in one year. If you sell a low-budget movie that is a WGA-approved film, and no other writers are hired to work on that film, then you will also earn more than most Americans earn in one year. Greed is a lot of fun, but it does not always lead to the right decision at the right time. Sometimes you have to give a little to get something else for the long run.

Selling a screenplay is not about the deal. The real deal is about getting your movie made in the best possible way. It is about telling your story. It is about getting that film credit. It is about building a career. It is about the wonder of movie-making.

If you concentrate on your craft of writing better screenplays and let your agent make your deals, deals will come and the money will follow.

WGA MINIMUM BASIC AGREEMENT "SHORT FORM CONTRACT"

The following contract is a format that is given out by the Writers Guild of America. It shows all of the important points that should be covered by any writing contract you receive. It is often called a "boiler plate" contract, meaning it covers all the basics for a deal.

DATE : _____

1. NAME OF PROJECT:_____ ("PROJECT")

2. NAME/ADDRESS OF COMPANY:

        _____("COMPANY")

        _____

        _____

3. NAME OF WRITER: _____("WRITER")

        SOCIAL SECURITY NUMBER _____

4. WRITER'S REPRESENTATIVE:_____

5. CONDITIONS PRECEDENT:
    ❑ W-4   ❑ I-9   ❑ OTHER, IF ANY

6. COMPENSATION:
    A. GUARANTEED COMPENSATION (SEE 11, BELOW): $ _____
    B. CONTINGENT COMPENSATION (SEE 11, BELOW): $ _____
    C. PROFIT PARTICIPATION: IF SOLE WRITING CREDIT, _____% OF (NET/GROSS) PROCEEDS; REDUCIBLE FOR SHARED CREDIT TO _____% (SEE 27, BELOW)

7. SPECIFIC MATERIAL UPON WHICH SERVICES ARE TO BE BASED, IF ANY (A COPY WILL BE SENT TO WRITER UNDER SEPARATE COVER):

8. OTHER WRITERS EMPLOYED ON SAME PROJECT OR FROM WHOM MATERIAL HAS BEEN OPTIONED/ACQUIRED, AND DATES OF MATERIAL, IF ANY:

9. COMPANY REPRESENTATIVE AUTHORIZED TO REQUEST REVISIONS:

10. COMPANY REPRESENTATIVE TO WHOM/PLACE WHERE MATERIAL IS TO BE DELIVERED:

11. SERVICES TO BE PERFORMED, INCLUDING NUMBER OF STEPS (*e.g., story and first draft, two rewrites and a polish*):

    A. FOR STEP 1:   ❑ GUARANTEED

                           ❑ OPTIONAL

          WRITING PERIOD: _____ WEEKS

          READING PERIOD: _____ WEEKS

          PAYMENT DUE: $_____

          (50% DUE ON COMMENCEMENT, 50% ON DELIVERY)

    B. FOR STEP 2 (IF APPLICABLE): ❑ GUARANTEED

                           ❑ OPTIONAL

          WRITING PERIOD: _____ WEEKS

          READING PERIOD: _____ WEEKS

          PAYMENT DUE: $_____

          (50% DUE ON COMMENCEMENT, 50% ON DELIVERY)

    C. FOR STEP 3 (IF APPLICABLE): ❑ GUARANTEED

                           ❑ OPTIONAL

          WRITING PERIOD: _____ WEEKS

          READING PERIOD: _____ WEEKS

          PAYMENT DUE: $_____

          (50% DUE ON COMMENCEMENT, 50% ON DELIVERY)

    D. FOR STEP 4 (IF APPLICABLE): ❑ GUARANTEED

                           ❑ OPTIONAL

          WRITING PERIOD: _____ WEEKS

          READING PERIOD: _____ WEEKS

          PAYMENT DUE: $_____

          (50% DUE ON COMMENCEMENT, 50% ON DELIVERY)

    E. FOR STEP 5 (IF APPLICABLE): ❑ GUARANTEED

                           ❑ OPTIONAL

          WRITING PERIOD: _____ WEEKS

          READING PERIOD: _____ WEEKS

          PAYMENT DUE: $_____

          (50% DUE ON COMMENCEMENT, 50% ON DELIVERY)

12. COMPANY SHALL PAY THE ABOVE GUARANTEED AMOUNTS DUE IF READING PERIODS PASS AND COMPANY DOES NOT REQUEST SERVICES; HOWEVER, IF THERE HAS BEEN NO INTERVENING WRITER(S), SERVICES SHALL BE DUE, SUBJECT TO WRITER'S PROFESSIONAL AVAILABILITY, FOR A PERIOD NOT TO EXCEED _____ MONTHS.

13. BONUS:

   A. For sole writing credit: $_____

   B. For shared writing credit: $_____
       Shared credit bonus will be paid on commencement of principal photography if no other writer has been engaged; balance to be paid on determination of writing credit.

   C. For "green light" or engagement of an "element": $_____
       If Writer is writer of record or is most recent writer on the Project at the time the Project is given a "green light" by a studio or an element is attached on a pay-or-play basis, Writer shall be given a bonus of _____ Dollars ($_____) which may ❑ may not ❑ be applied against the bonus in A. or B., above.

14. CREDITS AND SEPARATED RIGHTS:
   Per WGA MBA.

15. EXISTING CREDIT OBLIGATIONS REGARDING ASSIGNED MATERIAL, IF ANY (SUBJECT TO WGA MBA):

16. VIEWING CUT:
   Per WGA MBA: Writer shall be invited to view a cut of the film in time sufficient such that any editing suggestions, if accepted, could be reasonably and effectively implemented. Writer shall also be invited to [_____] other screenings.

17. PREMIERES:
   If writer receives writing credit, Company shall ❑ shall not ❑ provide Writer and one (1) guest with an invitation to the initial celebrity premiere, if held, with travel and accommodations at a level not less than the director or producer of the project.

18. VIDEOCASSETTE:
   Per WGA MBA.

19. TRANSPORTATION AND EXPENSES:
   If Company requires Writer to perform services hereunder at a location more than ____ miles from Writer's principal place of residence, which is _____, Writer shall be given first class (if available) transportation to and from such location and a weekly sum of $_____ ($_____ per week in a high cost urban area).

20. SEQUELS/REMAKES:

If separated rights,

- Theatrical sequels = 50% initial compensation and bonus; remakes = 33%.
- Series Payments: $ _____ per 1/2 hour episode; $ ____ per 1 hour episode; $ _____ per MOW (in network primetime or on pay television, otherwise $ _____ per MOW); $ _____ per sequel produced directly for the videocassette/videodisc market; $ _____ per product produced for the interactive market based on the Project; _____ [other, e.g., theme park attractions based on the Project].
- Spin-offs: Generic – 1/2 of above payments
                   Planted – 1/4 of above payments
- If Writer is accorded sole "Written by" or "Screenplay by" credit, Writer shall have the right of first negotiation on all audio-visual exploitation, including, but not limited to remakes and sequels and MOWs, mini-series and TV pilots (or first episode if no pilot) for a period of seven (7) years following release.

21. NOTICES:

All notices shall be sent as follows:

TO WRITER: TO COMPANY:

22. MINIMUM BASIC AGREEMENT:

The parties acknowledge that this contract is subject to all of the terms and provisions of the Basic Agreement and to the extent that the terms and provisions of said Basic Agreement are more advantageous to Writer than the terms hereof, the terms of said Basic Agreement shall supersede and replace the less advantageous terms of this agreement. Writer is an employee as defined by said Basic Agreement and Company has the right to control and direct the services to be performed.

23. GUILD MEMBERSHIP:

To the extent that it may be lawful for the Company to require the Writer to do so, Writer agrees to become and/or remain a member of Writers Guild of America in good standing as required by the provisions of said Basic Agreement. If Writer fails or refuses to become or remain a member of said Guild in good standing, as required in the preceding sentence, the Company shall have the right at any time thereafter to terminate this agreement with the Writer.

24. RESULTS AND PROCEEDS:

Work-Made-For-Hire: Writer acknowledges that all results, product and proceeds of Writer's services (including all original ideas in connection therewith) are being specially ordered by Producer for use as part of a Motion Picture and shall be considered a "work made for hire" for Producer as specially commissioned for use as a part of a motion picture in accordance with Sections 101 and 201 of Title 17 of the U.S. Copyright Act. Therefore, Producer shall be the author and copyright owner thereof for all purposes throughout the universe without limitation of any kind or nature. In consideration of the monies paid to Lender hereunder, Producer shall solely and exclusively own throughout the universe in perpetuity all rights of every kind and nature whether now or hereafter known or created in and in connection with such results, product and proceeds, in whatever stage of completion as may exist from time to time, including: (i) the copyright and all rights of copyright; (ii) all neighboring rights, trademarks and any and all other ownership and exploitation rights now or hereafter recognized in any Territory, including all rental, lending, fixation, reproduction, broadcasting (including satellite transmission), distribution and all other rights of communication by any and all means, media, devices, processes and technology; (iii) the rights to adapt, rearrange, and make changes in, deletions from and additions to such results, product and proceeds, and to use all or any part thereof in new versions, adaptations, and other Motion Pictures including Remakes and Sequels; (iv) the right to use the title of the Work in connection therewith or otherwise and to change such title; and (v) all rights generally known as the "moral rights of authors."

25. WARRANTY AND INDEMNIFICATION:

   A. Subject to Article 28 of the WGA Basic Agreement, Writer hereby represents and warrants as follows:

   1. Writer is free to enter into this Agreement and no rights of any third parties are or will be violated by Writer entering into or performing this Agreement. Writer is not subject to any conflicting obligation or any disability, and Writer has not made and shall not hereafter make any agreement with any third party, which could interfere with the rights granted to Company hereunder or the full performance of Writer's obligation and services hereunder.

   2. All of the Work (and the Property, if any) shall be wholly original with Writer and none of the same has been or shall be copied from or based upon any other work unless assigned in this contract. The reproduction, exhibition, or any use thereof or any of the rights herein granted shall not defame any person or entity nor violate any copyright or right of privacy or publicity, or any other right of any person or entity. The warranty in this subparagraph shall not apply to any material as furnished to Writer by Company (unless such furnished material was written or created by Writer or originally furnished to Company by Writer) or material inserted in the Work by Company, but shall apply to all material which Writer may add thereto.

   3. Writer is sole owner of the Property together with the title thereof and all rights granted (or purported to be granted) to Company hereunder, and no rights in the Property have been granted to others or impaired by Writer, except as specified, if at all, in this Agreement. No part of the property has been registered for copyright, published, or otherwise exploited or agreed to be published or otherwise exploited with the knowledge or consent of Writer, or is in the public domain. Writer does not know of any pending or threatened claim or litigation in connection with the Property or the rights herein granted.

   4. Writer shall indemnify and hold harmless Company (and its affiliated companies, successors, assigns, and the directors, officers, employees, agents, and representatives of the foregoing) from any damage, loss, liability, cost, penalty, guild fee or award, or expense of any kind (including attorney's fees (hereinafter "Liability") arising out of, resulting from, based upon or incurred because of a breach by Writer of any agreement, representation, or warranty made by Writer hereunder. The party receiving notice of such claim, demand or action shall promptly notify the other party thereof. The pendency of such claim, demand, or action shall not release Company of its obligation to pay Writer sums due hereunder.

   B. Company agrees to indemnify Writer and hold Writer harmless from and against any and all damages and expenses (other than with respect to any settlement entered into without Company's written consent) arising out of any third party claim against Writer resulting from Company's development, production, distribution and/or exploitation of the Project.

26. NO INJUNCTIVE RELIEF:

The sole right of Writer as to any breach or alleged breach hereunder by Company shall be the recovery of money damages, if any, and the rights herein granted by Writer shall not terminate by reason of such breach. In no event may Writer terminate this Agreement or obtain injunctive relief or other equitable relief with respect to any breach of Company's obligations hereunder.

27. PROFIT PARTICIPATION:

Terms to be negotiated in good faith. If the parties fail to reach agreement within [ ] months after execution hereof, either party, upon 30 days notice to the other, may submit the matter to what is known as a "baseball arbitration," in which each party presents one profit proposal and the arbitrator is required to adopt one of the two proposals. The arbitrator shall be selected and the arbitration conducted pursuant to the Voluntary Labor Arbitration Rules of the AAA.

28. AGREEMENT OF THE PARTIES:

This document [including Attachment 1, if any] shall constitute the agreement between the parties until modified or amended by a subsequent writing.

BY: _____   BY: _____
          [NAME OF WRITER]   TITLE

CC: WGA CONTRACTS DEPARTMENT

ATTACHMENT 1

ADDITIONAL PROVISIONS, IF ANY:

_____

_____

_____

_____

_____

_____

SAMPLE DEAL MEMORANDUM

Below are some of the major deal points in a *Deal Memorandum* for a writer's contract, negotiated by me, for a first-time sale of a new writer, for a high budget spec original screenplay. A Deal Memorandum is often drawn up, by the production entity or the agent, prior to the final contract and is the basis used for said contract. There are many more points included in most Deal Memorandums, but for our purposes, these are the most common and usual for all deals.

Date:
Subject: "Movie Title"
Writer: Jane Doe

MEMORANDUM OF AGREEMENT

The following are the terms of the agreement ("Agreement") between _____Studios ("Studio") and JANE DOE ("Writer") in connection with Studio's acquisition of all right, title and interest, including without limitation, all exclusive motion picture, television and allied and ancillary rights of every kind and nature, in and to the existing screenplay written by Writer entitled "MOVIE TITLE," including without limitation all versions and drafts thereof and all elements contained therein (collectively, the "Property"), in connection with a proposed theatrical motion picture tentatively entitled "MOVIE TITLE" (the "Picture").

    1. SCREENPLAY
      1.1 Purchase of Screenplay
        a. Grant of Rights. For good and valuable consideration (including, without limitation, that consideration set forth in Paragraph 1.4.a. (1) below), which consideration is hereby acknowledged by Writer to be sufficient, and which consideration shall be deemed in compliance with and inclusive of any and all minimum payments to which

Writer may be or may become entitled under the Writers Guild of America Minimum Basic Agreement ("MBA"), Writer hereby irrevocably and inclusively grants to Studio in perpetuity, throughout the universe all right, title and interest of any and every kind and nature, including without limitation, all motion picture, television, television series, sequel, remake, digital television, video and computer games, videocassettes and video or laser disc, any computer-related assisted media (including but not limited to CD-Rom, CD-I and similar disc systems, interactive media and multimedia and any other devices or methods now existing or hereinafter devised), in and to the Property. The foregoing grant of rights is made by Writer without any reservation of rights whatsoever. Without in any way limiting the foregoing, the rights granted by Writer to Studio shall include the copyright and all renewals and extensions of such copyright and all rights in the Property of every kind, nature or description, now or hereafter known, contemplated, developed, invented, devised or at any time coming into existence, including the exclusive, absolute and unlimited right to use the Property, and each and every part thereof, for any purposes in any manner whatsoever.

1.2.   <u>Warranties; Indemnity.</u> Writer hereby represents, warrants, and agrees that:

(a) The property was created and written by Writer and Writer is the author thereof and entitled to the copyright therein forever with the right to make such changes therein and such uses thereof as Writer may determine as author;

(b) The Property was written solely by and is original with Writer;

(c) To the best of Writer's knowledge or that which Writer

should know in the exercise of reasonable prudence, neither the Property nor any element thereof infringes upon any other literary properties;

(d) To the best of Writer's knowledge or that which Writer should know in the exercise of reasonable prudence, the production or exploitation of any motion picture or other production based on the Property will not violate the rights of privacy of any person or constitute a defamation against any person, nor will production or exploitation of any motion picture or other production based thereon in any other way violate the rights of any person whomsoever;

(e) To the best of Writer's knowledge or that which Writer should know in the exercise of reasonable prudence, Writer owns all rights in the Property free and clear of any liens, encumbrances, claims or litigation, whether pending or threatened;

(f) Writer has full right and power to make and perform this Agreement;

(g) Writer has not entered into any agreement prior to this Agreement with respect to the Property; and

(h) To the best of Writer's knowledge or that which Writer should know in the exercise of reasonable prudence, the Property has not previously been exploited as a motion picture, television production, play or otherwise, and no rights have been granted to any third parties to do so.

The term "person" as used herein shall mean any persons, firm, corporation or other entity.

II. <u>Additional Documentation</u>. Concurrently herewith, Writer will execute an assignment in the form of Exhibit "A" attached hereto and, at Studio's request, Writer will execute or cause the execution of any and all additional documents and instruments reasonably deemed by Studio to be necessary or desirable to effectuate the purposes of this Agreement. If Writer fails to sign and/or deliver to Studio any such document within ten (10) days of its delivery to Writer pursuant to Paragraph 5 below, Writer hereby appoints Studio as Writer's irrevocable attorney-in-fact to sign any such document on Writer's behalf, and Writer agrees that such appointment constitutes a power coupled with an interest.

III.   Consideration. In full consideration for the grant of rights in the Property to Studio hereunder and for all writing services by Writer in connection with the Picture as required by Studio, Writer shall be entitled to receive the total sum of $400,000 (the "Consideration").

(a) <u>Allocation of Consideration</u>.

(1) Unless increased pursuant to Paragraph 1.4.a. (2) below, an amount equal to $300,000 of the Consideration shall be deemed the purchase price for the acquisition of the rights in the Property;

(2) An amount equal to $1,000,000 of the Consideration shall be deemed an advance against the payment due Writer for Writer's writing services in connection with the Property, all of which writing services shall be performed for the minimum payment for the applicable writing step as required under the Writers Guild of American Theatrical and Television Basic Agreement (the "MBA"). To the extent that Studio requires Writer to perform writing services for which the total MBA Minimum Payment(s) for all required writing services would exceed said $100,000 amount, Studio shall pay the MBA Minimum Payment to Writer for said additional writing services. To the extent that Studio requires Writer to perform writing services for which the total MBA

Minimum Payment(s) for all required writing services is less than said $100,000 amount and the Actual MBA Minimum Payment shall be deemed as additional purchase price for the acquisition of the rights in the Property.

(b) <u>Payment of the Consideration</u>. The consideration set forth in Paragraph 1.4.a. above shall be payable to Writer as follows:

> (1) $300,000 upon Writer's execution and delivery to Studio of this Agreement;

> (2) $50,000 upon Writer's commencement of all writing services in connection with the Picture as requested by Studio;

> (3) $50,000 upon Writer's completion of writing services in connection with the Picture.

2. WRITING SERVICES AND COMPENSATION

2.1. <u>Writing Services – The Picture</u>. Writer shall render exclusive writing services in connection with the Picture as required by Studio during all writing periods. Writer shall commence such writing services and deliver the written material to Studio in accordance with the writing and delivery schedule(s) to be reasonably designated by Studio; provided that Writer shall write all additional writing step(s) within eighteen (18) months after the date of Writer's completion and delivery to Studio of the first writing step in connection with the Picture (or defer same pursuant to Paragraph 3.2 below) with each such additional step to be requested by Studio upon notice within four (4) weeks following Studio's receipt of the immediately prior writing step.

2.2 <u>Bonus</u>. If the Picture is produced as a theatrical motion picture and Writer receives sole screenplay credit upon final credit determination under the MBA, but not Article 7 of the theatrical Schedule A thereto ("Final Credit Determination"), then Writer shall be entitled to receive a cash bonus in the amount of $350,000, which bonus shall become payable upon Final Credit Determination. If the Picture is produced as a theatrical motion picture and Writer receives shared screenplay credit therefore upon Final Credit Determination, then in lieu of the foregoing, Writer shall be entitled to receive a cash bonus in the amount of $200,000, which bonus shall become payable upon Final Credit Determination. If the Picture is produced as a theatrical motion picture and Writer does not receive either sole or shared screenplay credit therefore upon Final Credit Determination, but provided that the Picture is based on the Property, then in lieu of the foregoing, Writer shall be entitled to receive a cash bonus in the amount of $100,000, which bonus shall be payable upon Final Credit Determination. Notwithstanding the foregoing, if upon commencement of principal photography no subsequent writers have been hired to render services in connection with the Picture, Writer shall be entitled to receive at such time the sum of $100,000 as an advance against any bonus payable to Writer under this Paragraph 2.2.

2.3 <u>Net Profits.</u> If the Picture is produced and released as a theatrical motion picture then Writer shall be entitled to receive contingent compensation:

> a. The flat sum of $100,000 at the point in time (if ever) that the Picture achieves Cash Breakeven (as defined below);
>
> b. If Writer receives sole screenplay credit for the Picture upon Final Credit Determination, Writer shall be entitled to receive an amount equal to 5% of 100% of the Net Profits, if any, of the Picture.
>
> c. If Writer receives shared screenplay credit for the Picture upon Final Credit Determination, then in lieu of the foregoing, Writer shall be entitled to receive contingent compensation in an amount equal to 2½% of 100% of the Net Profits, if any, of the Picture.

d. The following definitions shall apply to the provisions of this Paragraph 2.3:

(1) "Cash Breakeven" shall be defined as the end of the accounting period in which "Gross Receipts (as defined in Exhibit "NP" attached to the Agreement) first equal the aggregate of the following (which shall be deemed recoupable in the following order of priority:

a. An "off-the-top" Distribution Fee (as defined in Exhibit "NP") in the amount of 20% of all Gross Receipts;

b. All Distribution Costs as set forth in Paragraph IV of Exhibit "NP";

c. Accrued Interest as set forth in Paragraph V.C. of Exhibit "NP";

d. Overhead as set forth in Paragraph V.B. of Exhibit "NP";

e. The cost of Production as set forth in Paragraph V.A. of Exhibit "NP";

(2) Net profits shall be defined, computed and accounted in accordance with Exhibit "NP" (which includes a 15% overhead charge, plus charges for any Studio facilities used in accordance with Studios' then-current rate card) as modified solely by the Rider thereto, which is incorporated herein in its entirety by this reference.

e. Writer shall not be entitled to any such contingent compensation if Writer does not receive either sole or shared screenplay credit as set forth above.

3. GENERAL TERMS-WRITING SERVICES

3.1 <u>Exclusivity.</u> Writer's writing services hereunder shall be exclusive to Studio during all writing periods, and on a non-exclusive basis during all reading periods; providing that Writer's services on Writer's own account or for third parties shall not materially interfere with Writer's obligations hereunder. Time is of the essence respecting the writing services and delivery dates specified herein.

3.2 <u>Deferred Services.</u> Studio may defer Writer's services on any writing step to such other time as Studio elects (for a period up to 18 months, subject to suspension and extension for a period equal to any period Writer is unavailable to render services for Studio), subject only to Writer's unavailability due solely to conflicting professional contractual commitments; provided that upon notice from Studio, Writer shall be available to perform said writing services immediately after completion of the applicable writing steps for the prior contractual commitment. If Studio defers any writing step hereunder, Writer shall upon written request be entitled to the applicable payment for the applicable deferred writing services as if such deferred writing materials were timely ordered and timely delivered to Studio and as if the applicable reading and writing periods were fully utilized; provided, however, that if Writer defaults or reneges on his obligation to perform said services the advance paid to Writer shall be immediately repayable to Studio.

3.3 <u>Novelization</u>. Novelization shall be as set forth in the WGA MBA.

3.4 <u>Credit</u>. Credit shall be accorded as provided under the WGA MBA.

3.5 <u>First Opportunity</u>
<u>Theatrical Sequel or Remake.</u> For a period of seven (7) years after the initial release of the Picture, if Studio (or its assignees or licensees) elects, in its sole discretion, to produce or causes to be produced the initial theatrical sequel and/or initial theatrical remake based thereon (collectively, a "Theatrical Production"), and

if Writer receives sole screenplay credit on such original Picture upon Final Credit Determination and remains active as a writer in the motion picture industry at such time, Writer shall have the first opportunity to write such initial Theatrical Production (and each succeeding Theatrical Production provided that Artist received sole screenplay credit upon Final Credit Determination for the immediately preceding Theatrical Production) on terms to be negotiated in good faith (within Studio's usual parameters) but in no event on financial terms less favorable to Writer than herein; provided, however, that in the event no agreement is reached within thirty (30) days following Studio's service of notice on Writer of the commencement of negotiations, or if Writer elects not to write or is unavailable, Studio shall have the right to engage another writer(s) and shall have no further obligation to Writer with respect to such writing services hereunder except for the amounts (if any) to which Writer may be entitled pursuant to Paragraph 3.7. below.

3.6 <u>Television Production</u>. For a period of seven (7) years after the initial release (if any) of the Picture, if Studio (or its assignee or licensee) elects, in its sole discretion, to have written a teleplay for an initial television motion picture based on the Picture (i.e., a pilot, initial episode of a series, a movie-of-the-week or miniseries; collectively, a Television Production"), and if Writer received sole "screenplay by" credit upon final Credit Determination for the Picture and is then active as a writer in the theatrical and/or television motion picture industry and is available when and where required by Studio, then Studio shall first negotiate in good faith with Writer within Studio's standard parameters to engage Writer to write the teleplay for such initial Television Production based on the Picture. Writer's writing engagement in connection with the initial Television Production shall be subject to network, licensee or other broadcaster approval. If Studio and Writer fail to agree on terms for Writer's services in connection with such initial Television Production within thirty (30) days following Studio's service of notice on Writer of the commencement of negotiations therefore, or if Writer elects not to write or is unavailable, or Writer is not approved by the network, Studio shall have the right to engage another writer(s) and shall have no further obligation to Writer with respect to such writing services hereunder except for payments of royalties (if any) to which Writer may be entitled pursuant to Paragraph 3.7, below.

3.7 <u>Royalties</u>. If Studio (or its assignees or licensees) produces or causes to be produced a theatrical sequel to or theatrical remake of the Picture, and provided Writer received sole separation of rights under the MBA for the Picture and is not engaged to write for the applicable production described below, then Writer shall be entitled to the applicable royalty specified below. If Writer receives shared separation of rights under the MBA for the Picture and Writer is not engaged to write on the applicable production described below, then the applicable royalty set forth below shall be reduced by any royalty payable to a third party who shares such separated rights provided such royalty to Writer shall not be reduced by more than fifty percent (50%).

    (i) <u>Theatrical Sequel</u>. One-half of: (a) the cash compensation actually paid to Artist for acquisition of rights and writing services (i.e., the Consideration paid to Artist pursuant to paragraph 1.4 above); plus any sums earned as bonus compensation pursuant to Paragraph 2.2 above; and (b) the percentage of Net Profits, if any to which Writer was entitled for writing services on the Picture (e.g., 2½% of the Net Profits for the sequel if Writer received sole screenplay credit for the Picture).

(ii) <u>Theatrical Remake</u>. One-third of: (a) the cash compensation actually paid to Artist for acquisition of rights (i.e., the Consideration pursuant to Paragraph 1.4 above); plus any sums earned as bonus compensation pursuant to paragraph 2.2 above; and (b) the percentage of the Net Profits of such remake, if any, which percentage shall be equal to one-third of the percentage of Net Profits, if any, to which Writer was entitled for writing services on the Picture (e.g., 1.67% of the Net Profits for the remake if Writer received sole screenplay credit for the Picture).

(iii) <u>Television Series</u>. The following royalties are payable for each episode of a television series based upon the Picture produced for a particular broadcast season:

<u>Network Primetime</u>

<u>Running Time</u>

30 minutes (or less)	$1,750
60 minutes (but more than 30 minutes)	$2,250
90 minutes (but more than 60 minutes)	$2,900

(iv) <u>Reruns and Royalties</u>. Twenty percent (20%) of the applicable royalty set forth in subparagraph 3.7. (iii) shall be payable for each of the first five (5) network reruns in the combined territory of the U.S. and Canada. No further rerun payments shall be made thereafter.

J. <u>Movie-of-the-Week and Mini-Series</u>. $20,000 for the first two (2) hours and $10,000 for each additional hour thereafter (proratable for each partial hour), not to exceed a maximum of $80,000, regardless of running time.

(vi) <u>Time and Frequency of Payment</u>. Theatrical payments due under Paragraph 3.7. (iii) shall be payable on commencement of principal photography. Television payments shall be payable upon initial United States broadcast; provided, however, that if the applicable production is produced pursuant to an applicable buyer order, but not telecast, then the applicable royalty shall be paid within thirty (30) days after the end of the broadcast season for which it was ordered, provided that Studio has received the applicable license fee therefore.

(vii) <u>Inclusive of MBA Minimums.</u> The royalty and rerun payments set forth in Paragraph 3.7. (iii) are inclusive of the directly applicable minimum royalties and rerun fees payable under the MBA. Any additional payment required by the MBA under this or any other paragraph of this Agreement shall be payable at the minimum rate required under the MBA.

4. <u>MISCELLANEOUS [applicable to all writing services rendered by Writer pursuant to this Agreement]</u>

4.1 <u>Transportation and Expenses</u>. If Studio requires Writer to travel more than 50 miles from Writer's principal residence (presently Los Angeles County, California) in connection with Writer's services hereunder, then Writer shall be entitled to receive during such travel period a nonaccountable weekly proratable allowance (calculated at 1/7 thereof per day) in lieu of all living expenses or reimbursements in the amount of $1,750 in New York and London, $1,500 in other metropolitan areas (e.g. San Francisco), and $1,250 elsewhere and one round-trip air transportation, first-class, if available. In addition, if Writer is required to be on a distant location during principal photography of the Picture for longer than two (2) consecutive weeks, Writer shall be entitled to receive, on a one-time basis only, one (1) additional first-class round-trip transportation if available, and if used for Writer's non-business related companion to visit Writer at one such distant location. All travel arrangements, including but not limited to the acquisition of airline tickets, booking of accommodation, etc., shall be made through Studio's location or travel department unless prior written approval is obtained from a Studio business affairs executive. Studio shall not be responsible for any other expenses or perquisites of Writer.

4.2 <u>Ownership and Distribution.</u> The results and proceeds of Writer's services hereunder in connection with the Picture shall be deemed a work-made-for-hire specially ordered or commissioned by Studio. Studio shall exclusively own all now known and/or hereafter existing rights of every kind throughout the universe, in perpetuity and in all languages, pertaining to such results and proceeds, the Picture, and all elements therein for all now known and/or hereafter existing uses, media, and forms, including, without limitation, all copyrights (and renewals and extensions thereof), all forms of: motion picture, television, digital television, video and computer games, videocassette and video or laser disc, any computer-assisted media (including, but not limited to CD-Rom, CD-I and similar disc systems, interactive media and multi-media and any other devices and/or methods now existing and/or hereinafter devised), character, sequel, remake, theme park, stage play, sound record, merchandising and all allied, and all ancillary and subsidiary rights therein, and the foregoing is inclusive or a full assignment to Studio thereof.

4.3 No Obligation to Use. Studio is not obligated to use the services of Writer or to develop, produce, distribute, or exploit the Picture, or, if commenced, to continue the development, production, distribution, or exploitation of the Picture in any territory. Regardless of whether or not Studio elects to produce, distribute and/ or exploit the Picture (or to commence same), Studio is not obligated to use the services in whole or in part of Writer hereunder, subject only to Studio's obligation to pay sums owed and accrued hereunder.

●●●

There are many more points in most contracts; however, the above are the most important in connection with the writer's fees, bonuses, ownership, and rights. A Net Profit definition would also be attached as well as points on insurance, indemnifications, etc.

> EXERCISES

1. Upon reading the above Agreement(s), learn the terminology and become familiar with the important points of the deal.

2. Read a few issues of the *Hollywood Reporter* and *Daily Variety*. See if you can now determine the veracity of the announcement of writer deals/script sales.

3. In these Agreements note that amounts paid as "bonuses" are dependent upon screen credit received by Writer(s).

$ THE MONEY $

20

Everyone wants to know about the money in Hollywood. Whether they are in the business or not, people love to hear about the huge paydays of movie stars, directors, and even writers. Magazines and newspapers print the box-office tally for the day, week, month, and even the year for each major motion picture. The ubiquitous television entertainment news shows love to tell all about the flops and the hits in terms of the dollars involved. Yes, we all love the stories about money and feel that the pot of gold is at the end of a screenplay road.

Well, that's true and it's not true. The depth of that pot of gold can vary widely. The financial aspects of writing depend on many elements.

FACTORS DETERMINING A WRITER'S PAYDAY

Here are some of the major factors that determine how much money you, as a professional writer, might be paid for your services on a film or TV project:

Writer's WGA Membership

Whether you are a member of the WGA or not, you will most likely be working for a company that is a signatory of the WGA Minimum Basic Agreement (see Chapter 19). The WGA has a listed amount of minimums that any company must pay to writers who are members of the Guild at the time their deal is made. If the writer has an agent then the overall monies are usually increased by at least 10% of the WGA fee, so that the writer's payment is never less then that WGA minimum.

Production Company's WGA Signatory Status

If you are a member of the WGA you are not allowed to work for companies that are not signed up with the WGA. They must sign an agreement stating that they will follow all of the WGA-defined rules and regulations that are set in place to protect writers. In the event you are a new writer, without any credits, and you sell a project to a non-signatory production company, you are able to negotiate any deal you wish. These are usually fairly low-budgeted films.

Proposed Film's Overall Budget

When the picture in development is planned and budgeted as an expensive movie, the writer is likewise going to get a bigger payday. If the film planned is a medium- or low-budgeted picture, then the writer's fee will go down accordingly. All of the aforementioned pre-supposes that the writer and producer are signed with the WGA.

Writer's Last Fee for a Movie Deal

If you have sold one or two movies within the past three to five years, it is likely that your next film writing deal will garner you a larger payday. Each movie fee is based on the previous movie fee and often gets you a raise. Most of the time your agent will be able to negotiate a bump in your salary. Remember that these fees are still tied to the budget of the new script or assignment. If your new project is a much lower-budgeted film, your new deal will not bring in higher fees.

How Much a Writer's Work Is Wanted

Just like any other industry, the movie business is a slave to supply and demand. If you are thought to be the very best writer to be hired for a project or if your spec script is exactly what the producer wants to make, then you are in the cat-bird's seat and will likely get a very nice payday. In the event that you happen to hit the nail on the head and write a spec script that is just what the studio needs, then you, or your agent, will be able to negotiate a high figure.

Auctions

This is where the business gets very exciting. When more than one company wants your spec script or your writing services at a given time, the situation becomes known as an *auction*. The companies will bid for you and/or your spec. The egos involved at the studio level are enormous so they will pay almost anything to get what they want. That is to say that they consider it a "win" to get the project away from other bidders. The heat and energy involved in these auction negotiations with your agent can be electrifying.

Size of the Producing Entity

There has been a lot of talk about the smaller paydays for everyone in the business because of the world economy, at the time of the publication of this book. It's true that some of the fees negotiated for writers have decreased (but to no less than the WGA minimums), and that at this moment there are few bidding wars on spec scripts. However, you will see that even these lesser amounts are very high when compared to the average salary of an American worker for one year of employment. The big studios have the ability to pay big dollars if they want a specific writer or project. Major motion picture studios will also pay more for a screenplay if it is a high-budgeted film with lots of stunts and expensive action sequences. Independents are in a different category in that they are constantly trying to keep costs down. The independent production entities usually produce low- or medium-budget films, and the script price is lowered accordingly.

Is a Distributor in Place?

Having a major distribution arm in place for a company is an important factor. If the company knows they can successfully release a movie, they have a great comfort zone.

Television Deals

When it comes to writing for episodic television series, all of the prices are fixed and firm. There is no negotiation. The prices paid to writers are established via the Writers Guild as well as the amounts to be paid for re-runs and residuals, if you have created a show.

The following are the WGA minimums for television writers for sitcoms, dramas, two-hour movies, and miniseries. You will note that there are built-in increases for the years 2010 and 2011.

WGA 2008 THEATRICAL AND TELEVISION BASIC AGREEMENT
TELEVISION COMPENSATION

NETWORK PRIME TIME (ABC, CBS, FBC and NBC)

Length of Program:	**15 minutes or less**		
Applicable minimums	Effective 2/13/08- 5/1/09	Effective 5/2/09- 5/1/10	Effective 5/2/10- 5/1/11
STORY+	$ 3,926	$ 4,044	$ 4,165
TELEPLAY	9,534	9,820	10,115
Installments:			
+ First Draft:	90% of minimum or 60% of Agreed Compensation, whichever is greater		
Final Draft:	Balance of Agreed Compensation		
STORY & TELEPLAY	11,795	12,149	12,513
Installments:			
+ Story:	30% of Agreed Compensation		
First Draft Teleplay:	The difference between the Story Installment and 90% of minimum, or 40% of Agreed Compensation, whichever is greater		
Final Draft Teleplay:	Balance of Agreed Compensation		

Length of Program:	**30 minutes or less**		
STORY+	$ 7,196	$ 7,412	$ 7,634
TELEPLAY	15,482	15,946	16,424
Installments:			
+ First Draft:	90% of minimum or 60% of Agreed Compensation, whichever is greater		
Final Draft:	Balance of Agreed Compensation		
STORY & TELEPLAY	21,585	22,233	22,900
Installments:			
+ Story:	30% of Agreed Compensation		
First Draft Teleplay:	The difference between the Story Installment and 90% of minimum, or 40% of Agreed Compensation, whichever is greater		
Final Draft Teleplay:	Balance of Agreed Compensation		

+On pilots only, the writer is to be paid 10% of the first installment (as an advance against such first installment) upon commencement of services.

The applicable minimum for a pilot is 150% of the applicable minimum set forth above.

$ THE MONEY $

WGA 2008 THEATRICAL AND TELEVISION BASIC AGREEMENT
TELEVISION COMPENSATION

NETWORK PRIME TIME (ABC, CBS, FBC and NBC)

Length of Program: **60 minutes or less**

Applicable minimums	Effective 2/13/08- 5/1/09	Effective 5/2/09- 5/1/10	Effective 5/2/10- 5/1/11
STORY+	$12,668	$13,048	$13,439
TELEPLAY	20,886	21,513	22,158

Installments:
+ First Draft: 90% of minimum or 60% of Agreed Compensation, whichever is greater
Final Draft: Balance of Agreed Compensation

STORY & TELEPLAY	31,748	32,700	33,681

Installments:
+ Story: 30% of Agreed Compensation
First Draft Teleplay: The difference between the Story Installment and 90% of minimum, or 40% of Agreed Compensation, whichever is greater
Final Draft Teleplay: Balance of Agreed Compensation

Length of Program: **90 minutes or less**

STORY+	$16,925	$17,433	$17,956
TELEPLAY	30,094	30,997	31,927

Installments:
+ First Draft: 90% of minimum or 60% of Agreed Compensation, whichever is greater
Final Draft: Balance of Agreed Compensation

STORY & TELEPLAY	44,668	46,008	47,388

Installments:
+ Story: 30% of Agreed Compensation
First Draft Teleplay: The difference between the Story Installment and 90% of minimum, or 40% of Agreed Compensation, whichever is greater
Final Draft Teleplay: Balance of Agreed Compensation

+On pilots and one-time programs 90 minutes or longer, the writer is to be paid 10% of the first installment (as an advance against such first installment) upon commencement of services.

The applicable minimum for a pilot is 150% of the applicable minimum set forth above.

Television movies have a fixed rate that may be negotiated, if you are a very highly sought after writer. The WGA also has minimums for tv movies in the event you are selling your first spec.

WGA 2008 THEATRICAL AND TELEVISION BASIC AGREEMENT
TELEVISION COMPENSATION

NETWORK PRIME TIME (ABC, CBS, FBC and NBC)

Length of Program: **120 minutes or less** (but more than 90 minutes)
NON-EPISODIC[#]

Applicable minimums	Effective 2/13/08- 5/1/09	Effective 5/2/09- 5/1/10	Effective 5/2/10- 5/1/11
STORY+	$24,665	$25,405	$26,167
TELEPLAY	42,135	43,399	44,701

Installments:
+ First Draft: 90% of minimum or 60% of Agreed Compensation, whichever is greater
Final Draft: Balance of Agreed Compensation

STORY & TELEPLAY	64,238	66,165	68,150

Installments:
+ Story: 30% of Agreed Compensation
First Draft Teleplay: The difference between the Story Installment and 90% of minimum, or 40% of Agreed Compensation, whichever is greater
Final Draft Teleplay: Balance of Agreed Compensation

Length of Program: **120 minutes or less** (but more than 90 minutes)
EPISODIC

STORY+	$22,601	$23,279	$23,977
TELEPLAY	38,613	39,771	40,964

Installments:
+ First Draft: 90% of minimum or 60% of Agreed Compensation, whichever is greater
Final Draft: Balance of Agreed Compensation

STORY & TELEPLAY	58,772	60,535	62,351

Installments:
+ Story: 30% of Agreed Compensation
First Draft Teleplay: The difference between the Story Installment and 90% of minimum, or 40% of Agreed Compensation, whichever is greater
Final Draft Teleplay: Balance of Agreed Compensation

+On pilots and one-time programs 90 minutes or longer, the writer is to be paid 10% of the first installment (as an advance against such first installment) upon commencement of services.

#The applicable minimum for a pilot is 150% of the applicable *non-episodic* minimum set forth above.

In the final analysis I feel that professional writers are very well paid for their work. Some of the amounts I was able to negotiate for my clients for feature films were astronomical and some were simply very good. Writers have a tendency to complain about what they are paid, but they are doing the work they love for fees that most people would kill for. Here are the WGA minimums for low and high budget feature films:

WGA 2008 THEATRICAL AND TELEVISION BASIC AGREEMENT
THEATRICAL COMPENSATION+

		Third Period Effective 5/2/10-5/1/11	
		LOW	HIGH
A.	Original Screenplay, Including Treatment	**$62,642**	**$117,602**
	Installments:		
	Delivery of Original Treatment	28,382	47,000
	Delivery of First Draft Screenplay	24,668	47,000
	Delivery of Final Draft Screenplay	9,592	23,602
B.	Non-Original Screenplay, Including Treatment	**54,814**	**101,936**
	Installments:		
	Delivery of Treatment	20,554	31,334
	Delivery of First Draft Screenplay	24,668	47,000
	Delivery of Final Draft Screenplay	9,592	23,602
C.	Original Screenplay, Excluding Treatment **or** Sale/Purchase of Original Screenplay	**42,088**	**86,156**
	Installments for Employment:		
	Delivery of First Draft Screenplay	32,505	62,667
	Delivery of Final Draft Screenplay	9,583	23,489
D.	Non-Original Screenplay, Excluding Treatment **or** Sale/Purchase of Non-Original Screenplay	**34,251**	**70,489**
	Installments for Employment:		
	Delivery of First Draft Screenplay	24,668	47,000
	Delivery of Final Draft Screenplay	9,583	23,489
E.	Additional Compensation for Story included in Screenplay	7,837	15,667
F.	Story or Treatment	20,554	31,334
G.	Original Story or Treatment	28,382	47,000
H.	First Draft Screenplay, with or without Option for Final Draft Screenplay (non-original)		
	First Draft Screenplay	24,668	47,000
	Final Draft Screenplay	16,440	31,334
I.	Rewrite of Screenplay	20,554	31,334
J.	Polish of Screenplay	10,283	15,667

+Explanation of discounts on page 1.

There are many more points of information in the Writers Guild Minimum Basic Agreement. This Agreement as well as a plethora of other important information about writers fees, rights, residuals, re-run payments, etc., is available to you at: *www.wga.org.*

● ● ●

These are just some of the factors involved in your deals. The bottom line is that all deals are good and most likely your paydays will get better and better over time. As long as you and your material are excellent, you will never go hungry. There is and always has been a constant thirst for new material and new writers. This will never change.

> **EXERCISES**

1. Call the WGA for explanations of anything you don't understand in those deals.

2. Read about recent movie screenplay deals on the Internet.

3. In the trades, see if you can find articles about writers who are hired on to rewrite someone else's screenplay.

HOW WAS MY MEETING?

21

Once you cross that distant threshold and finally get an agent, your whole writing life will change dramatically. You will now start a completely new phase of your writing career.

PRELIMINARY STEPS

This new phase begins with the *submissions* process and is closely followed by the *meetings* process of this new world. Obviously this agent has taken you on as a client because you have at least one great new screenplay that he or she feels he or she can set up somewhere. To this end the agent begins submitting that screenplay with a great deal of hype about what a tremendous "find" you are.

Now here comes the *waiting* aspect for you. It's torture, there's no denying that. It is ten times worse than waiting to hear from a writing contest, because this is the real thing. Those Hollywood insiders with the power to actually make something happen are now looking at your script.

Try your best not to bug your agent every five minutes to see if he or she has heard from anyone. Believe me, if there's good news, your agent will be on the phone or emailing you immediately.

BASICS OF MEETINGS

Good news can be interpreted in many ways. Certainly the best news is that some huge mainstream producer and major studio wants to put your film on the fast track and produce it right away. If only life were that simple. Let's be realistic. Good news in Hollywood most often means that people have liked your work and want to:

a. meet with you;

b. read something else that you've written;

c. pass the script up the ladder in their company; and/or

d. present your script to a studio or two or three.

All of these are terrific. Don't even try to judge which one is better for you. You must have "meet and greet" meetings. These meetings give you the chance to get writing assignments. They give you the opportunity to bond with development executives and producers who will need writers. They also give you the chance to pitch your original script ideas and that may lead to a development deal wherein you are paid to write your own project.

You must have original pitch ideas in the same genre as the script that you've set up. People in the industry like to know that you are not a "one-shot" writer. In other words if you've written a murder mystery and they need someone to do a rewrite in the same genre, they'll want to read another similar writing sample.

When it comes to a first meeting that is set up by your agent you will need to know if it is a *pitch* meeting, or a *meet and greet* meeting, or a meeting to discuss your screenplay and possible changes to it. Your agent will know what they want; however you must be prepared for all of the above. It is very rare for your agent or manager to attend meetings with you so you will be in this meeting alone unless you have a writing partner.

You will also need to know exactly whom you are meeting. This means finding out who the people are in the hierarchy of their particular company. Are you going to be meeting with a low-level development executive or a vice-president of development or the head of the company? In any case these people are all important to your career. I have watched many, many low-level development people become heads of studios or major producers in a very short time. They are wonderful contacts because they also are very well connected to other development people in film. They share information about new writers and projects. Hopefully they will be talking about you. If that happens your agent will begin getting lots of calls about reading your work.

PREPARING FOR MEETINGS

Preparing yourself for your meetings should be an easy task. After all you are the creative person and this is your work that you'll be discussing. No one knows it as well as you. Here's the rub. Can you think on your feet?

These people will throw you some curves that you never expected. They will have their own ideas as to how you should change your beloved screenplay. They will make suggestions that appear to you to be insane or stupid. You will have to learn to listen closely. Try to figure out if this is just creative talk or if they really want you to do these changes. The job of development people is to *develop* someone's work. That means they must find ways to change your script or they won't be doing their job. There is no perfect screenplay. Sometimes changes must be made to suit a director the company has in mind, or to cast a specific actor, or to appeal to a certain demographic. You may not ever really know why these changes are requested. It's best to listen with an open mind. You can certainly argue your point; however, it won't be good for you to be intransigent and belligerent with these people. They hold your future in their hands.

Are you able to listen to criticism? Quite often development people and producers have great ideas that would make your script much more interesting to the studio or their financing entities. You might feel as if your work is being attacked when they toss out criticism. These people are used to having their own way and they can be very tough. Weigh your options while listening to their words. Do you really want to walk out of their office in a huff, or do you want to sell your movie and get it made? It may be emotionally traumatizing, but you must hang in there to get the job done. They probably won't ask you to add a zombie to your romantic comedy, but they will have some very odd-sounding ideas.

167

Keep in mind it is also permissible to tape your meetings. Simply explain that you don't want to forget anything and put the recording device right out there on the desk, coffee table, or anywhere that works.

PITCHING IN MEETINGS

Next these folks will want to know what else you've written and if you have any ideas for forthcoming screenplays. Hopefully you've taken steps to learn how to pitch a story. Your agent is at your disposal to help you learn this skill and there are consultants, books, magazine articles, and seminars to assist you further. This is a skill that is crucial. Remember that this is a fast and furious business. Most producers have the attention span of a gnat. Once they lose their concentration, you are dead. Keep your pitches short and to the point. Watch to see if your listener's eyes are glazing over.

WHEN A MEETING IS OVER

The aforementioned leads me to explain how you know when the meeting is over. You may actually be having the time of your life. Here you are in a big, beautiful office that's bedecked with giant posters of films that have been produced by these amazing people. You are drinking their wonderful coffee or French water that has been served to you by servile employees. You are discussing your manuscript with important people who really understand film. It can be a fabulous experience.

Warning! Don't overstay your welcome. Again remember that these are very busy people.

An average meeting lasts thirty minutes, give or take. Watch for the inevitable signs that the meeting is finished (See Chapter 15). Are they still really listening to you? Is the person behind the desk starting to take calls? Is he or she shuffling papers on his or her desk? If you see these things starting to happen, it is incumbent upon you to make your good-byes. If the people you are meeting with want you to stay they will let you know in no uncertain terms.

●●●

I spent many years watching various clients ace meetings or destroy their careers in meetings. Be willing to share your ideas and to pay keen attention to theirs. Quid pro quo. It is a two-way street. Meetings are give-and-take endeavors.

After it's over don't forget to call your agent and tell him or her all about it. It will give your agent the knowledge he or she needs to take the next step for you.

> **EXERCISES**

1. Practice pitching your next project ideas.

2. Write short, one- or two-page synopses of your ideas to leave behind at your meetings.

3. Map out your way to your meeting place so you won't be late.

THE PRICE OF BEING A WRITER: ARE YOU WORTH IT?

22

Becoming a writer will cost you financially, personally, and emotionally. You will constantly need new and improved computers, cell phones, text messaging, copiers, and all sorts of technological paraphernalia that will inevitably require upgrading. You will need more paper, toner, lighting, repairs to desks, shelves, bookcases, and the car. You will run out of room in your home office and have to deal with space issues.

Writing at home or even in a rented office will cost you emotionally as well as financially. Your neighbors will be too noisy or too quiet. New writers should spend a lot of money on going to writers' events (conferences, pitch fests, film festivals). These events are well worth the investment, which will cover the costs of airfare, hotels, event fees, and food.

Often there are fees to enter screenwriting contests and competitions.

Here are the actual percentages (of the 100% gross you will receive) of what you will have to pay for the pleasure of being paid as a professional writer:

Agent	10%
Personal manager	10%
Lawyer	5%
Business Manager	5%
IRS	33% to 49%
Ex-spouse	?%
Child support	?%
You	?%

Then there is a price you will pay for being different. You will pay a social price for not having the nine-to-five career your friends and family expect of you. Your parents, your spouse, and even your children may not understand your choices and their lack of emotional support may cost you dearly.

You will likely be doing odd little jobs to sustain yourself while you try to become a professional writer. Or perhaps you will have another career that will require your attention. Splitting your time and energy between this outside work and writing will cost you emotionally, as you spend years laboring so hard at your scripts while generating no income from your chosen craft. If you are blessed and cursed with a need and talent to write, you must have a strong inner core to persevere. You will often have to remind yourself that this is your choice, that this is something you love, and that this is a talent you cannot waste.

From the first time you sit down at that computer or take pen and legal pad in hand to begin your first screenplay, you will have a long and winding journey. Always remember that the brass ring in this business is really gold and that you must keep pursuing your dream. The rewards of working as a professional writer are wonderful. You will experience great joy when you see those movies that you have written up on a film screen with a crowded audience. You will know the happiness of making movies and entertainment that may last throughout history.

You are an artist with a gift. Be proud of that gift and keep moving toward your goal. Tell your stories. Someday you may entertain and enlighten millions. You may bring joy, laughter, tears, and excitement into the lives of people all over the world.

DON'T GIVE IT AWAY

23

As you struggle to become a professional screenwriter, someone inevitably will ask you to write a project for free. The decision whether to do this is not as simple as it may appear at first glance.

If you are a member of the Writers Guild of America, you are not allowed to write for free, so there is no problem. However, for new writers it is a real temptation. After all, what's the harm? You might think that maybe it will sell and then you'll get paid. You might think that it would be a great experience, that this producer will "owe you." There are so many thoughts running around in your head telling you that you should do this favor, which might turn into a real bonanza for you. Stop right there.

Writers are infamous for doing their best to put off writing what they should be writing. We all want to extend our deadlines and go to Starbuck's instead of sitting alone in that room at the computer. When someone comes along and wants to work with you on a project it will sound good primarily because you won't be working alone in a vacuum. You'll feel that you are in a business partnership, when in reality you are just being used.

WHY WORKING FOR FREE IS A BAD IDEA

At some point a wannabe producer or even a well-known producer will beg you or try to entice you to write a project for him for free. Producer X will tell you that you will be paid when it is sold. He might tell you that he has backers and/or financiers who are interested in the idea. He will tell you how hot the project will be as soon as you write it. What he won't do is pay you. "What," you may ask, "is the problem with this?" You may think, "I'm already writing on spec so what could be the harm?"

This is not a good idea for the following reasons:

• **You will not own your own work.**

This is the biggest problem and the most difficult to overcome. If there is a reversion clause in the agreement that you have with this producer, it will imply that you will own it after everyone in town has already looked at the script and that the producer will be attached forever. If, by some lucky chance you do find a buyer for the project after it reverts to you, the original producer may ask for an exorbitant amount of money and an on-screen title in an inappropriate place. This may very well quash the deal for you and kill the project.

• **The producer will have the right to bring in any number of other writers to rewrite your script.**

This means that your original drafts may be changed so much that you may not even recognize your own work and because of this you may not receive that coveted production bonus that you were promised.

• **Invariably the producer will want you to do rewrites and polishes without payment.**

They will blackmail you with the threats of using other writers.

• **You will be spending a lot more time than you originally expected on this project and at the end you will not have the right to show it to anyone because you will not own it.**

• **Your time is much better spent writing original material, going to writers' conferences, going to film festivals, reading books on screenwriting, going to places and events that will help you to network with other writers, etc.**

- **The producer may not feel that he or she owes you anything.**

    You may be just another writer in a series of writers used on this project.

- **If the producer wants a script for free, it usually means that he or she is not a professional and will try to use your work to get into the industry.**

- **In the unlikely event that this project does sell, you will not be in the position to get much out of it, unless you have a hard and fast contract upfront.**

- **Because you will be working on a project that is not your own original idea, it will not be a good writing sample for you.**

    You will have spent all of that time and effort and good will with nothing to show for it at the end of the day.

- **If you feel that you can protect your rights with a contract, then you will incur attorney's fees.**

    This will make the situation a truly lopsided arrangement for you.

WORKING WITH SCRIPT CONSULTANTS 24

You are the lucky ones. You are members of a club that has only existed for about twenty-five years. This club consists of potential professional screenwriters and television writers who have the opportunity to avail themselves of professional help in their writing endeavors.

Writers have certainly become successful without the use of consultants but it is a hard and circuitous road. Trying to find out what you really have is almost impossible on your own or by way of your friends' opinions. Even film-school teachers are not always privy to what is being sought by the studios, nor do they often know what subject matter might be very cold.

WHAT SCRIPT CONSULTANTS OFFER

You need a professional consultant to find out if your script is as good as you think. They can help you with problems in the plot, structure, characters, etc. that you may not have seen. Consultants should also know if, by current industry standards, your material's subject matter is hot or cold. They should be clear in their critiques of your work and available for future questions. These pros are invaluable in identifying where you might have gone astray in your plotting or story. They should be able to lead you back to the right route to make your script better.

Since becoming a script and novel consultant I have worked with many wonderful writers who have made some decisions in their early drafts that may have seemed correct at the moment, but that led the story or characters into the wrong directions. It's my job to see this and to help rectify the problem. A consultant finds not only what is right about your script, but also what is wrong and how it can be fixed. It's not an easy job and you need to find a real pro with whom to work.

Taking classes and reading the books on writing are important but you cannot really know about your projects until a consultant has read them. It's a huge mistake to submit material before it is ready for industry professionals. If they see a problem on page 3, the script is tossed out. There are no second chances. There is so much material being submitted that no one has the time or interest in seeing your scripts after reading one that was not very good. Producers and studio execs want and have a right to expect very professionally written projects.

Screenplay consultants are dispassionate about you and your work; therefore we are able to judge the material on its own merits.

THE PRICE OF EXPERIENCE

Script consultants come in all shapes and sizes. They have varying backgrounds and abilities. Their fees are wildly disparate. This means that you must do your due diligence to find the right person for you. Use the Internet to check the backgrounds of consultants. Find out if their history is worthwhile for you. For example, if a consultant has spent most of her early career in the television business and is now touting herself to feature film writers, you should probably look elsewhere. Trust your instincts when it comes to deciding if the consultant doesn't have the right credentials. Look at their websites. You might even want to call and double-check any connections they mention.

Because I became a screenplay consultant after twenty-five years as a literary agent, I bring some additional benefits to my clients. While working on their scripts, not only do I delve into the characters, plot, structure, and dialogue, but I also know the marketplace and the major players in Hollywood. After living so closely with new and professional writers for such a long time, I have an affinity for their trials and tribulations and understand the difficulties that they face by trying to get into the inner-world of movie-making. I know what works and what doesn't work. I know how to improve the work and along the way am able to offer advice and counsel on their future careers. It's a great job and I love doing it.

After researching all of those consultants, you will be faced with the problem of payment. Since the fees are so different it will be difficult to decide whom to choose. It is not always the case that you get what you pay for. Sometimes consultants with medium-sized fees can be better for you than the most expensive ones. It is a bit of a crap-shoot. Read their material carefully to see what you will be getting for each fee. I had a client with whom I had worked on several screenplays. She called with a new project. She told me that she had found another consultant who charged a very, very low fee. I looked up that particular consulting service and discovered that the fee she mentioned was only for "coverage." *Coverage* is merely a synopsis of your script and possibly the consultant's opinion of its saleability. Writers don't need coverage; they already know what their script is about. This writer needed much more hands-on work from a consultant. If I hadn't checked this consultant out this client would have wasted money and been sorely disappointed.

Package Deals

Many consultants include packages in their price lists. This means that you may pay for them to work on a treatment, and screen-play, plus one or two rewrites or some variation of this. They usually work it out so that if you pay the package price it will be less expensive than paying for each step individually. I even know one consultant who charges a one-year consulting fee and it's huge. When you first start working with a consultant I feel it would be best to do a one-step process first by sending him or her one script. This way you can see whether this is the right relationship for you. You may find that the consultant makes unclear suggestions for changes, or doesn't offer concrete solutions to your problems, or is hard to reach. If these or any other problems surface, you may decide to move along to some-one else.

● ● ●

Whether you work with me or any of my colleagues in the field, you have a great opportunity to enhance your work with a screenplay consultant. Please avail yourself of this terrific option.

(IV) GETTING GOING

WELCOME TO THE BEGINNING
OF YOUR CAREER

25

I have written this book to help you realize your dreams. The advice, true stories, copies of contracts, warnings, and my personal opinions and experiences are here to assist you in your quest for that gold ring of success in the entertainment business. None of this great info will work if you don't practice your writing skills and continue to improve them.

You will need to write, write, write, then rewrite, rewrite, rewrite and then start all over again. I understand how hard writing is but I also understand how much fun it is. There's nothing like the great feeling of finishing a wonderful product and having it recognized for its true value.

You will need a great deal of self-confidence to move forward through the trials and tribulations of creating a big career in film and/ or TV. You'll need to remind yourself constantly that this is what you want and this is what you deserve. Information is power and the information here is just the beginning of the multitude of things you are going to learn as you meander down this fascinating road.

Tenacity is another big word in my life and should be in yours. My grandmother used to call it *stick-to-itiveness.* That's a silly word for a very important trait. Don't give up and don't give in. You may not see it immediately but you may have a great talent — it just takes lots of time and effort to discover that place within yourself. So batten down your hatches and keep going.

A support system of some sort will also be invaluable to you. Find one or make one. It doesn't matter if they are fellow writers or family members or just one person who is always on your side. It is necessary to have people in your life who believe in you and will support your dreams and desires. Keep them close and be sure to return their love as they keep sustaining you.

Don't believe anyone who tells you to quit. It may take a lot of time and energy and dedication to become a good writer. No one is perfect in the beginning of a career. Writing is a process without an end date.

Continuing to learn the craft of writing is essential. Take more classes, go to film school, and buy books that will add to your understanding of the job of writing. Subscribe to screenwriters' magazines and go on the Internet for more and more information.

If you are not watching movies then you aren't doing your job. Old movies, new movies, large-scale, major-studio, tent-pole films, independents, and foreign films will help you to become a better screenwriter. Analyze these films and discuss them with friends. Try to figure out why some movies are wonderful and meaningful and some are entertaining and fulfilling while some just don't seem to work.

Knowledge is power so give yourself that gift. If I can help you, then please email me (see About the Author) and I'll be happy to do what I can to aid you in your process.

I've loved every minute of my work in the entertainment world. It's never failed to entertain me. There have been so many wonderfully fascinating people with amazing ideas who have populated my life. I am profoundly grateful for these years of experiences. It has always been a wild ride.

Most important of all is to remember to have some fun with this exciting, creative, challenging, and rewarding business of show!

Ⓥ GENERAL INFORMATION

FAQS

AGENTS AND CLIENTS

Who needs an agent?

Every writer who wants to work as a professional in the film and television industry.

What does an agent look for in you?

A consistently productive writer with a positive outlook.

Do you wait for the right one?

It's difficult to know after one or two meetings if an agent is the perfect match for you. Once you sign with your first agent, time and experience will prove whether your choice was a good one.

What's the ideal communication between agent and client?

You have a right to know what your agent is doing on your behalf. You need to clearly state your aims and desires and always let the agent know what you are working on.

WHAT HOLLYWOOD IS REALLY LIKE

What range of experiences can I look forward to?

Just like the Clint Eastwood movie, you will find the good, the bad, and the ugly. A few bad experiences must not stop you from moving forward. Some of your choices may not work out but there are many, many chances to succeed. The highs are so high that you will never experience anything quite so great. Selling a script, getting a writing assignment, being hired to adapt a great book, seeing your name on a movie screen and in the newspaper ads are just some of the fabulous things that will come your way. You also have the potential to make huge sums of money to do what you want to do and what you love to do: write.

Does Hollywood really run on rumors?

Show business is rife with constant rumors and gossip. It sometimes feels as if we feed off of it. I've always loved hearing who was doing what to whom and all of the other little tidbits of information that are being bandied about town. It is a sideline of everyone in the business. Somehow info always leaks out and it is part of all of our jobs to know exactly what's happening at all times.

What's it like for women in the business?

It's still a bit harder to be a woman than a man in a writing career. That is not to say it is anywhere near impossible. If you have the goods, it doesn't matter if you are a green elf — the Hollywood community will find you and want you.

What kind of power do writers have?

Unfortunately the rumors are true that writers have little or no power. They are the often unrewarded and unsung heroes of the business. You will have to find your gratification elsewhere.

Is ageism an issue in Hollywood?

The skinny on this is that when a new screenplay arrives at the desk of an executive he or she doesn't know the age, religion, or political preference of the author. After your first meeting the cat's out of the bag, so to speak. Hopefully your attitude and ideas will be contemporary and positive.

How do you separate what's phony from what's real?

We have an overabundance of both. My advice is to beware of the phonies and try to build those relationships with people who are real and honest in their dealings.

What's the role of the trades?

The trades are always filled with great rumors as well as some truths about what is happening on any given day. We all read them faithfully, but with a grain of salt. A "Million Dollar Sale" is rarely true. However, the trades can tell you if your newest best friend has just been fired or hired.

Is there a lot of lying in Hollywood?

First, be aware that everyone exaggerates in this town. After that comes the lying. When there is so much money and power involved in a business it's difficult to escape the lies that are being told. I've always worked on the premise that my word is my bond and that, like Superman, I never lie. I find that telling the truth is not only the right thing to do but it also happens to be the easiest thing to do.

Do I move up or move out?

Yes, it's very hard to tread water in such a competitive world. Keep honing your craft, keeping finding fresh ideas, keep making new friends. There's always a pack of others who are trying desperately to get your job.

Am I hot or not?

I've watched the most successful writers fall from grace and never be able to get back up. It's so easy to fail. One or two bad or even mediocre scripts and you can lose your credibility. If you are too difficult to work with and don't listen to the powers that be, you will get a bad reputation and the rumor mill will track it all over town. Strive to keep your reputation clean and your writing at its best.

PUBLICITY

How important is publicity in Hollywood?

Promotion and publicity are always positive. Someone once said, "I don't care what they say about me as long as they spell my name right." I pretty much adhere to this philosophy. People constantly need to be reminded about you and your work. They need to know that you've sold a script or changed agencies or been hired to write something. If you can get it in the trades, go for it.

RESULTS

WEBSITES

The Writers Guild of American (West or East)

www.wga.org

Research site for:

     a. rules

     b. contracts

     c. minimums

     d. screen credit/arbitration

     e. committees

     f. general information for writers

The American Film Institute

www.afi.com

Research site for:

     a. film history

     b. classes

     c. competitions

The Great American Pitch Fest

www.pitchfest.com

Great place to network, learn, and pitch to industry executives.

www.Developmenthell.net

Lots of good information here.

Scriptwriters Network

www.scriptwritersnetwork.org

They present great speakers every month.

Storylink

www.storylink.com

A good site for mingling with other writers.

Shaw's Guide to Writers' Conferences and Workshops

writing.shawguides.com

Here you will find all the workshops, conferences, and film festivals that will help your career.

The Hollywood Creative Directory

www.hcdonline.com

The best reference book in town.

Internet Movie Database

www.IMDb.com

The best movie and movie-industry research site.

Independent Writers of Southern California

www.iwosc.org

An excellent organization with lots of guest speakers.

SUGGESTED READING

Chitlik, Paul. *Rewrite*.
Studio City, CA: Michael Wiese Productions, 2008.

DiMaggio, Madeline. *How to Write for Television*.
New York: Fireside, 2008.

Edwards, Rona & Skerbelis, Monika. *I Liked It, Didn't Love It: Screenplay Development from the Inside Out*.
Beverly Hills, CA: ESE, 2009.

Fong-Yoneda, Kathie. *The Script Selling Game*.
Studio City, CA: Michael Wiese Productions, 2002.

Goldman, William. *Adventures in the Screen Trade*.
New York: Grand Central Publishing, 1989.

Gregory, Mollie. *Women Who Run the Show*.
New York: St. Martin's Press, 2002.

Hauge, Michael. *Writing Screenplays That Sell*.
New York: Harper Perennial, 1991.

Marks, Dara. *Inside Story*.
Studio City, CA: Three Mountain Press, 2007.

Seger, Dr. Linda. *Making a Good Script Great*.
Los Angeles: Samuel French, 1994.

Snyder, Blake. *Save the Cat!*
Studio City, CA: Michael Wiese Productions, 2005.

Vogler, Christopher. *The Writer's Journey.*
Studio City, CA: Michael Wiese Productions, 2007.

HOLLYWOOD TERMINOLOGY

adaptation: a script based on another form of original work such as a novel, play, or research material. An adaptation may be from the writer's own work or another person's project.

character arc: the personal growth of the main character in a screenplay.

coverage: a report written by a reader for use by an agent, producer, or studio executives. It is a synopsis of the material along with the reader's opinion of its worth as a future motion picture or television project.

development deal: similar to an *overall deal.*

development executives: people working for motion picture or television studios, or television networks, or production companies, whose job it is to read every draft the writers generates and to give notes and/or changes to each draft.

dramedy: a dramatic piece that has comedic overtones.

genre: the type of story, plot, screenplay, or teleplay, e.g., action-adventure, drama, comedy, etc.

Hollywood: used in this book to denote the entertainment business in all of its aspects. This includes the people as well as the business and the geographical location.

newbie: an unsold writer.

notes meeting: an opportunity for a screenplay's purchaser to discuss the project and offer opinions to the writer as to how the script should be changed.

novel rights: authorization that must be obtained by a writer who wants to write an adaptation of a novel and have the ability to sell said adaptation in screenplay form. The writer must request this directly from the novel's publisher and/or author.

on-screen credit: the "Written by… " credit seen on either a television or a motion picture screen.

original screenplay: a script generated from an original idea.

overall deal: an agreement between a writer and a production company wherein the writer works exclusively for said production company to develop projects.

paid ads: all advertisements for a film, placed in newspapers, magazines, posters, etc., and paid for by the production entity.

pitches: short verbal synopses of a writer's project. They may be anywhere from three to thirty minutes in length.

pitch fests: events wherein writers present their projects to professionals in the entertainment business.

player: anyone in Hollywood who is working successfully in the mainstream.

polish: a minor rewrite.

query letter: a letter sent by a writer to an agent or producer to see if he or she will read the writer's scripts.

rewrite: an overhaul of an original screenplay's first draft, or subsequent drafts.

rom-com: a romantic comedy.

screenplay consultant: a person hired to review a script and prescribe ways of improving the project.

script doctor: a person hired to review a script and prescribe ways of improving the project.

spec script: an original screenplay that is written without financial backing.

synopsis: a written version of the story of a screenplay. It should be between two and three pages in length.

teleplay: a screenplay written specifically for television use.

tent pole: any large-scale feature film, financed by a major studio, that the studio believes will do a huge opening business.

third-party financiers: companies and/or persons who add additional financing to a motion picture or television project.

Tinseltown: a Hollywood term denoting all of Hollywood as it applies to the entertainment business.

trades: the news periodicals specific to the entertainment business, e.g., the *Hollywood Reporter* and *Variety*.

treatment: a written version of the story of a screenplay. It should be between ten and twenty-one pages long.

INDEX

A

Adaptation 50, 195–196
AMC 51
APA 95
Attorney 100, 109, 128, 144
Auction 157

B

Blockbuster 51
Bloom, Mel 21
Bootsie 130
Booty Call 130
Braun, Zev 36
Budget   28, 47, 84, 132–133, 141, 156–157, 161
Business manager 1, 171

C

CAA 95
Character arc 9, 11, 195
Clooney, George 26
Commissions 61, 102, 122–123, 133
Consultant 1, 6–7, 39, 45, 66, 70, 76, 91, 177–180, 197, 201

H

I

J

L

M

ABOUT THE AUTHOR

Photo Credit: John Strand Photography, Woodland Hills, CA

MICHELE WALLERSTEIN was a literary agent for twenty-five years and now works as a screenplay, novel, and career consultant. In these capacities, she helps writers get their work into shape so that it is marketable to the Hollywood community and/or the publishing world. Michele started reading at age four and never stopped. She also fell in love with the movies as a very young child and continues to be a huge fan. She lives in Sherman Oaks, California, with her husband, Gregg Weiss. Gregg is a high school teacher in Covina, where he teaches at-risk and learning disabled students.

Michele has been a guest speaker at numerous film festivals, pitch festivals, and writers' groups all across the U.S. She teaches the ins and outs of the business as well as how to get the most out of your material. She is prominently listed, interviewed, and quoted in numerous books, newspapers, and articles on the entertainment business.

Michele served as executive vice-president of Women in Film and was on its Board of Directors for many years. She was a member of the Agents' Advisory Board for *Creative Screenwriting* magazine. She is a member of the Academy of Television Arts and Sciences and has served on their Blue Ribbon voting panel for the Emmy Awards. She has proudly been a pioneer and great supporter of the progress of women's careers in all fields. Her web address is *www.novelconsultant.com* and you can email her at *novelconsult@yahoo.com*.

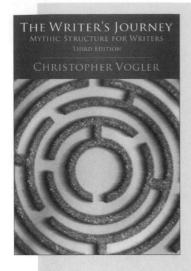

THE WRITER'S JOURNEY – 3RD EDITION
MYTHIC STRUCTURE FOR WRITERS

CHRISTOPHER VOGLER

BEST SELLER
OVER 180,000 COPIES SOLD!

See why this book has become an international best seller and a true classic. *The Writer's Journey* explores the powerful relationship between mythology and storytelling in a clear, concise style that's made it required reading for movie executives, screenwriters, playwrights, scholars, and fans of pop culture all over the world.

Both fiction and nonfiction writers will discover a set of useful myth-inspired storytelling paradigms (i.e., "The Hero's Journey") and step-by-step guidelines to plot and character development. Based on the work of Joseph Campbell, *The Writer's Journey* is a must for all writers interested in further developing their craft.

The updated and revised third edition provides new insights and observations from Vogler's ongoing work on mythology's influence on stories, movies, and man himself.

"This book is like having the smartest person in the story meeting come home with you and whisper what to do in your ear as you write a screenplay. Insight for insight, step for step, Chris Vogler takes us through the process of connecting theme to story and making a script come alive."
> – Lynda Obst, Producer, *Sleepless in Seattle, How to Lose a Guy in 10 Days*;
> Author, *Hello, He Lied*

"This is a book about the stories we write, and perhaps more importantly, the stories we live. It is the most influential work I have yet encountered on the art, nature, and the very purpose of storytelling."
> – Bruce Joel Rubin, Screenwriter, *Stuart Little 2, Deep Impact,*
> *Ghost, Jacob's Ladder*

CHRISTOPHER VOGLER is a veteran story consultant for major Hollywood film companies and a respected teacher of filmmakers and writers around the globe. He has influenced the stories of movies from *The Lion King* to *Fight Club* to *The Thin Red Line* and most recently wrote the first installment of *Ravenskull*, a Japanese-style manga or graphic novel. He is the executive producer of the feature film *P.S. Your Cat is Dead* and writer of the animated feature *Jester Till*.

$26.95 · 448 PAGES · ORDER NUMBER 76RLS · ISBN: 9781932907360

CINEMATIC STORYTELLING
THE 100 MOST POWERFUL FILM CONVENTIONS
EVERY FILMMAKER MUST KNOW

JENNIFER VAN SIJLL

BEST SELLER

CINEMATIC STORYTELLING

THE 100 MOST POWERFUL FILM CONVENTIONS EVERY FILMMAKER MUST KNOW JENNIFER VAN SIJLL

How do directors use screen direction to suggest conflict? How do screenwriters exploit film space to show change? How does editing style determine emotional response?

Many first-time writers and directors do not ask these questions. They forego the huge creative resource of the film medium, defaulting to dialog to tell their screen story. Yet most movies are carried by sound and picture. The industry's most successful writers and directors have mastered the cinematic conventions specific to the medium. They have harnessed non-dialog techniques to create some of the most cinematic moments in movie history.

This book is intended to help writers and directors more fully exploit the medium's inherent storytelling devices. It contains 100 non-dialog techniques that have been used by the industry's top writers and directors. From *Metropolis* and *Citizen Kane* to *Dead Man* and *Kill Bill*, the book illustrates — through 500 frame grabs and 75 script excerpts — how the inherent storytelling devices specific to film were exploited.

You will learn:
· How non-dialog film techniques can advance story.
· How master screenwriters exploit cinematic conventions to create powerful scenarios.

"Cinematic Storytelling *scores a direct hit in terms of concise information and perfectly chosen visuals, and it also searches out... and finds... an emotional core that many books of this nature either miss or are afraid of."*
— Kirsten Sheridan, Director, *Disco Pigs*; Co-writer, *In America*

"Here is a uniquely fresh, accessible, and truly original contribution to the field. Jennifer van Sijll takes her readers in a wholly new direction, integrating aspects of screenwriting with all the film crafts in a way I've never before seen. It is essential reading not only for screenwriters but also for filmmakers of every stripe."
— Prof. Richard Walter, UCLA Screenwriting Chairman

JENNIFER VAN SIJLL has taught film production, film history, and screenwriting. She is currently on the faculty at San Francisco State's Department of Cinema.

$24.95 · 230 PAGES · ORDER NUMBER 35RLS · ISBN: 9781932907056

SELLING YOUR STORY IN 60 SECONDS
THE GUARANTEED WAY TO GET
YOUR SCREENPLAY OR NOVEL READ

MICHAEL HAUGE

BEST SELLER

Best-selling author Michael Hauge reveals:
- · How to Design, Practice, and Present the
  60-Second Pitch
- · The Cardinal Rule of Pitching
- · The 10 Key Components of a Commercial Story
- · The 8 Steps to a Powerful Pitch
- · Targeting Your Buyers
- · Securing Opportunities to Pitch
- · Pitching Templates
- · And much more, including "The Best Pitch I Ever Heard," an exclusive collection
  from major film executives

"Michael Hauge's principles and methods are so well argued that the mysteries of effective screenwriting can be understood — even by directors."

> — Phillip Noyce, Director, *Patriot Games, Clear and Present Danger,*
> *The Quiet American, Rabbit-Proof Fence*

"... one of the few authentically good teachers out there. Every time I revisit my notes, I learn something new or reinforce something that I need to remember."

> — Jeff Arch, Screenwriter, *Sleepless in Seattle, Iron Will*

"Michael Hauge's method is magic — but unlike most magicians, he shows you how the trick is done."

> — William Link, Screenwriter & Co-Creator, *Columbo; Murder, She Wrote*

"By following the formula we learned in Michael Hauge's seminar, we got an agent, optioned our script, and now have a three-picture deal at Disney."

> — Paul Hoppe and David Henry, Screenwriters

MICHAEL HAUGE is the author of *Writing Screenplays That Sell*, now in its 30th printing, and has presented his seminars and lectures to more than 30,000 writers and filmmakers. He has coached hundreds of screenwriters and producers on their screenplays and pitches, and has consulted on projects for Warner Brothers, Disney, New Line, CBS, Lifetime, Julia Roberts, Jennifer Lopez, Kirsten Dunst, and Morgan Freeman.

$12.95 · 150 PAGES · ORDER NUMBER 64RLS · ISBN: 9781932907209

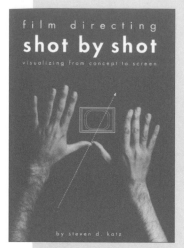

FILM DIRECTING: SHOT BY SHOT
VISUALIZING FROM CONCEPT TO SCREEN

STEVEN D. KATZ

BEST SELLER
OVER 200,000 COPIES SOLD!

Film Directing: Shot by Shot — with its famous blue cover — is the best-known book on directing and a favorite of professional directors as an on-set quick reference guide.

This international bestseller is a complete catalog of visual techniques and their stylistic implications, enabling working filmmakers to expand their knowledge.

Contains in-depth information on shot composition, staging sequences, visualization tools, framing and composition techniques, camera movement, blocking tracking shots, script analysis, and much more.

Includes over 750 storyboards and illustrations, with never-before-published storyboards from Steven Spielberg's *Empire of the Sun*, Orson Welles' *Citizen Kane*, and Alfred Hitchcock's *The Birds*.

"(To become a director) you have to teach yourself what makes movies good and what makes them bad. John Singleton has been my mentor... he's the one who told me what movies to watch and to read Shot by Shot."
— Ice Cube, *New York Times*

"A generous number of photos and superb illustrations accompany each concept, many of the graphics being from Katz' own pen... Film Directing: Shot by Shot *is a feast for the eyes."*
— *Videomaker* Magazine

"... demonstrates the visual techniques of filmmaking by defining the process whereby the director converts storyboards into photographed scenes."
— *Back Stage Shoot*

"Contains an encyclopedic wealth of information."
— *Millimeter* Magazine

STEVEN D. KATZ is an award-winning filmmaker and also the author of *Film Directing: Cinematic Motion*.

$27.95 · 366 PAGES · ORDER NUMBER 7RLS · ISBN: 9780941188104

THE POWER OF THE DARK SIDE
CREATING GREAT VILLAINS
AND DANGEROUS SITUATIONS

PAMELA JAYE SMITH

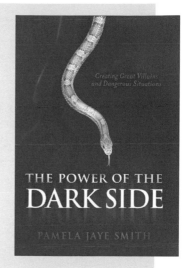

Who doesn't love the Dark Side? Darth Vader, Cruella De Vil, Tony Soprano — everybody loves a great villain. And every story needs dramatic conflict — internal and external — to really resonate. This comprehensive, accessible book gives you tools to craft the most despicable villains in your stories.

Conflict is the very heart and soul of drama. Mythologist Pamela Jaye Smith's latest book explores character conflict and a multitude of ways to achieve it:

· Defining the Dark Side helps you select and clarify the worldview that influences your characters' actions.

· The Three Levels of the Dark Side — personal, impersonal, and supra-personal — offer layers of interweaving conflict.

· A roll-call of Villains includes Profiles and Suggestions for creating your own versions of reader's bad-to-the-bone favorites.

· Learn to match Antagonists to Protagonists, and to use the Sliding Scale of Evil.

"The Power of the Dark Side *is an incredible exploration of the different dimensions of Evil. Pamela Jaye Smith demonstrates once again that she is one of the world's experts, not only on multi-cultural mythology but also on the application of the ideas of archetype, symbol, and cognitive science. While she's written this book with the writer in mind, her exploration of the ideas of evil will be of great value to teachers, therapists, and anyone who deals with people, education, motivation, or persuasion. For writers, it opens up a world of ideas that will help in building more complex antagonists. To have a great hero, you need a great villain.* Dark Side *delivers far more than you'd expect from one book.*"
> — Rob Kall, publisher of *OpEdNews.com* and founder, Storycon Summit Meeting on the Art, Science and Application of Story

PAMELA JAYE SMITH is an international speaker, consultant, writer, award-winning producer-director, and founder of MYTHWORKS *www.mythworks.net*. Credits include Microsoft, Paramount, Disney, Universal, GM, Boeing, the FBI and US Army. Smith has authored the MWP book, *Inner Drives*. She has taught writers, directors, and actors at USC, UCLA, American Film Institute, RAI-TV Rome, Denmark, France, New Zealand, Brazil, and many other venues.

$22.95 · 266 PAGES · ORDER NUMBER 82RLS · ISBN 13: 9781932907438

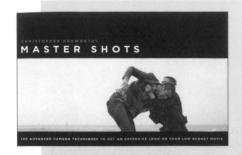

MASTER SHOTS
100 ADVANCED CAMERA TECHNIQUES TO GET AN EXPENSIVE LOOK ON YOUR LOW BUDGET MOVIE

CHRISTOPHER KENWORTHY

Master Shots gives filmmakers the techniques they need to execute complex, original shots on any budget. By using powerful master shots and well-executed moves, directors can develop a strong style and stand out from the crowd. Most low-budget movies look low-budget, because the director is forced to compromise at the last minute. *Master Shots* gives you so many powerful techniques that you'll be able to respond, even under pressure, and create knock-out shots. Even when the clock is ticking and the light is fading, the techniques in this book can rescue your film, and make every shot look like it cost a fortune.

Each technique is illustrated with samples from great feature films and computer-generated diagrams for absolute clarity.

Use the secrets of the master directors to give your film the look and feel of a multi-million-dollar movie. The set-ups, moves and methods of the greats are there for the taking, whatever your budget.

"Master Shots *gives every filmmaker out there the blow-by-blow setup required to pull off even the most difficult of setups found from indies to the big Hollywood blockbusters. It's like getting all of the magician's tricks in one book."*
— Devin Watson, Producer, *The Cursed*

"Though one needs to choose any addition to a film book library carefully, what with the current plethora of volumes on cinema, Master Shots *is an essential addition to any worthwhile collection."*
— Scott Essman, Publisher, *Directed By* Magazine

"Christopher Kenworthy's book gives you a basic, no holds barred, no shot forgotten look at how films are made from the camera point of view. For anyone with a desire to understand how film is constructed — this book is for you."
— Matthew Terry, Screenwriter/Director, Columnist
www.hollywoodlitsales.com

Since 2000, CHRISTOPHER KENWORTHY has written, produced, and directed drama and comedy programs, along with many hours of commercial video, tv pilots, music videos, experimental projects, and short films. He's also produced and directed over 300 visual FX shots. In 2006 he directed the web-based Australian UFO Wave, which attracted many millions of viewers. Upcoming films for Kenworthy include *The Sickness* (2009) and *Glimpse* (2011).

$24.95 · 240 PAGES · ORDER NUMBER 91RLS · ISBN: 9781932907513

THE MYTH OF MWP

In a dark time, a light bringer came along, leading the curious and the frustrated to clarity and empowerment. It took the well-guarded secrets out of the hands of the few and made them available to all. It spread a spirit of openness and creative freedom, and built a storehouse of knowledge dedicated to the betterment of the arts.

The essence of the Michael Wiese Productions (MWP) is empowering people who have the burning desire to express themselves creatively. We help them realize their dreams by putting the tools in their hands. We demystify the sometimes secretive worlds of screenwriting, directing, acting, producing, film financing, and other media crafts.

By doing so, we hope to bring forth a realization of 'conscious media' which we define as being positively charged, emphasizing hope and affirming positive values like trust, cooperation, self-empowerment, freedom, and love. Grounded in the deep roots of myth, it aims to be healing both for those who make the art and those who encounter it. It hopes to be transformative for people, opening doors to new possibilities and pulling back veils to reveal hidden worlds.

MWP has built a storehouse of knowledge unequaled in the world, for no other publisher has so many titles on the media arts. Please visit www.mwp.com where you will find many free resources and a 25% discount on our books. Sign up and become part of the wider creative community!

Onward and upward,

Michael Wiese
Publisher/Filmmaker